With every purposeful step away from her Leo took, the hope and excitement whipping through her system withered that little bit more, deflating her by the second.

Would Willow meet someone like him ever again? Someone who had such an extraordinarily intense effect on her? It didn't seem likely. Men like him didn't grow on trees.

So why was she standing here like a lemon?

Why wasn't she going after him and telling him she wanted more?

What was she *doing*?

She had nothing to lose and everything to gain from pursuing the passion she'd just experienced. Who cared if they were as different as two people could be? She wasn't after a happy-ever-after with him. She wasn't after that with *anyone*. She just wanted one night.

Lucy King spent her adolescence lost in the glamorous and exciting world of Harlequin when she really ought to have been paying attention to her teachers. But as she couldn't live in a dreamworld forever, she eventually acquired a degree in languages and an eclectic collection of jobs. After a decade in southwest Spain, Lucy now lives with her young family in Wiltshire, England. When not writing or trying to think up new and innovative things to do with mince, she spends her time reading, failing to finish cryptic crosswords and dreaming of the golden beaches of Andalucia.

Books by Lucy King

Harlequin Presents

Stranded with My Forbidden Billionaire

Passionately Ever After...
Undone by Her Ultra-Rich Boss

Passion in Paradise
A Scandal Made in London

Lost Sons of Argentina
The Secrets She Must Tell
Invitation from the Venetian Billionaire
The Billionaire without Rules

Visit the Author Profile page
at Harlequin.com for more titles.

Lucy King

VIRGIN'S NIGHT WITH THE GREEK

PAPL
DISCARDED

✦HARLEQUIN
PRESENTS

HARLEQUIN®
PRESENTS™

Recycling programs
for this product may
not exist in your area.

ISBN-13: 978-1-335-58437-3

Virgin's Night with the Greek

Copyright © 2023 by Lucy King

For questions and comments about the quality of this book,
please contact us at CustomerService@Harlequin.com.

Harlequin Enterprises ULC
22 Adelaide St. West, 41st Floor
Toronto, Ontario M5H 4E3, Canada
www.Harlequin.com

Printed in U.S.A.

VIRGIN'S NIGHT WITH THE GREEK

PROLOGUE

'SHE'S DOING *WHAT*?'

In response to the bombshell his younger sister had just dropped, Leonidas Stanhope sank into the chair behind his vast glass desk, his stomach tightening and his head already beginning to throb in a horribly familiar way.

'She's having herself painted,' Daphne repeated dully in Greek as she stared out of the window at the view of London that stretched out far below in the late May sunshine. 'In the nude. For Lazlo. As a birthday present, she said. He's turning seventy next week.'

'Seventy?'

'I know,' said Daphne. 'I can only assume he's a fan of Botox. I don't know why she couldn't simply have gift-wrapped a voucher for some more of that.'

'That would have been far too subtle.'

As his sister muttered her agreement, Leo

closed his eyes and pinched the bridge of his nose even though he knew perfectly well it would alleviate precisely nothing. He'd been firefighting his mother's scandals for years, ever since he'd become the head of the family following his father's sudden death twelve years ago, when he was nineteen. Some were huge, some were minor, all were exhausting.

Was there to be no end to the drama the woman caused? She was approaching sixty. At what age would dignity kick in and give him a break? No time soon, by the sound of things.

With a sigh, he fought the urge to grind his teeth, pulled himself together and redirected his attention to this latest incident. 'I thought she and Lazlo had parted ways.'

Daphne turned from the window to take a seat on the other side of the desk. 'That was two months ago,' she said despondently, flopping back against the leather the colour of whisky. 'They've since reconciled. She told me she was missing the sex.'

Leo winced.

'The portrait's to be part of an exhibition by up-and-coming young British artists at the Tate Modern. In a fortnight. Three days before my wedding. Can you believe it?'

'Unfortunately, I can,' he said, stifling a sigh

of exasperation. 'All too easily. She's so self-absorbed, I doubt the timing of it would even have crossed her mind. Or the appropriateness.'

'It'll hit the press,' Daphne continued, her voice becoming increasingly tremulous as her dark eyes began to shimmer. 'The tabloids will have a field day. And the photos… God. Everyone at our wedding will be talking about it and gawping at her. As if the outfit she's planning on wearing isn't bad enough. I mean, white. Really? I don't think I can stand it, Leo. I don't know what to do. How do we stop it? Ari has no metaphorical weight to throw around and you know what Mama thinks of him. He begged her to at least hold off for a few more weeks, but she just said she wasn't being dictated to by a waiter and hung up on him.'

'I can imagine,' he muttered, jaw clenched.

'So can *you* do something about it?'

Of course he could. Fixing problems and managing people was a large part of what he did, whether as CEO of the Stanhope Kallis banking and shipping empire or as the protective eldest sibling of a large, much-loved tribe.

But more to the point, he *would* do something because even if he was neither of those individuals, he could never have ignored the rawness in his sister's voice. The tears and pain she was trying to suppress sliced at his chest like a knife, and a white-hot wave of frustrated anger surged through him.

Daphne had overcome so much to get to this point. Eight years ago, at the age of fourteen, she'd been diagnosed with acute myeloid leukaemia. She'd subsequently spent more time in hospital than out of it. She'd had blood transfusions and battled infections. She'd undergone rounds of chemotherapy and radiotherapy and suffered all the grim side effects that went with that. The initial prognosis had not been good, but despite this she'd never lost her optimism. She'd smiled her way through the most gruelling of times.

And so even though she'd eventually beaten the odds and been in remission for three years now, the outlook as positive as it could be, and even though he'd never understand the attraction of romantic love with all the hideous emotion and chaos that seemed to inevitably come with it, Leo would allow absolutely nothing to overshadow a day no one had ever thought they'd see.

'Leave it with me.'

CHAPTER ONE

BENEATH THE SPARKLING surface of the gorgeously cool water, Willow Jacobs reached the end of the granite-lined pool, executed a lazy tumble turn and emerged with barely a splash to set off on another leisurely length of crawl.

The water slipped over her body like liquid pain relief. The heat of the Greek early summer sun warmed her skin like a balm. With every stroke, the tension in her hands that spread up her arms and into her shoulders and back while she worked eased. With every kick, the twinges and aches that came from sitting in one position for too long dispersed like watercolours in the rain.

She'd been working on and off for nearly a month now, with only one five-day break, which hadn't been much of a break, but she didn't resent the ten-hour days in the slightest. How could she when she was producing the best painting of her life? From the moment she'd put pastel to paper, the lines had come swiftly and the form had taken shape organically, as if her hands and fingers required no conscious input on her part at all.

Willow knew the rare and precious alchemy didn't stem from her environment, luxurious and comfortable though it was. Nor was it attributable to a sudden surge of talent because she already had that in abundance. It came entirely from her subject, who was as charmingly fascinating as she was utterly self-centred.

Not only was the raven-haired, sloe-eyed Selene Stanhope exquisitely beautiful and in possession of a spectacular body that belied her age and the six children she'd borne, she was also a Greek socialite who'd lived an adventurous, glitzy life. When she wasn't grumbling about her eldest son, about how disappointingly staid and repressed he was, about how it was his sole mission in life to pop up and spoil her fun, she liked to reminisce. At length. The stories she regaled made her sparkle and glow, and it was this inner radiance that gave the portrait such unique luminescence and vibrancy.

In that respect, it was a shame the it was nearly finished, Willow reflected as she bumped up against the wall and turned again.

She could sit and listen to Selene's exploits for ever. Parties that culminated in literal swinging from the chandeliers. Holidays on private Caribbean islands in the company of glamorous celebrities. The clothes, the extravagance, the men…

The tales were enviably bold, colourful and passionate. Bittersweet, too, since they brought back memories of Willow's own mother, who'd died a decade ago and had been the polar opposite. And while she could see they might prove a challenge to an apparently stiff upper-lipped and emotionally barren son, they offered a tantalising glimpse into an exotic aristocratic world that a solidly middle-class, permanently broke Willow would never inhabit.

On the other hand, completion of the painting meant payment. It meant framing and packaging and shipping the piece to an exhibition that she could never have dreamed of being able to contribute to.

Having her work on such prominent and illustrious display would bridge the gap between struggling artist and success. It would bring in more, perhaps even better commissions, which would establish an exciting career she adored and provide the versatility she needed to be able to manage the endometriosis that had such a massive impact on how she lived her life.

So while her time at the villa in Kifissia was coming to an end, it was a cause for celebration rather than regret. She'd always be grateful to Selene for expressing an interest in her over the canapés at the London event at which she'd been waitressing to supplement her income, and taking a chance on her. Thanks to her current client's openness and connections, Willow's future stretched out before her, brighter and more hopeful than ever before. Barring some catastrophe, it was secure. After years of upheaval, of learning how to manage the monthly agony while trying to break into the tightly knit art world and make a living, everything was finally coming together.

As the significance of this sank in properly for the first time, relief surged through her, so immense that it quickened her pulse and tightened her lungs. Her head spun and her limbs went weak. Dizzy, losing her buoyancy, Willow mistimed her breath and inhaled a lungful of pool water. She spluttered. Coughed. Flailed. She dipped beneath the surface for a moment but was just about pop up again and regain control of the situation when she was suddenly buffeted by a wave, grabbed from behind and hauled against something hard.

Shock and panic slammed into her. Adrenalin flooded her system. Instinctively, she squirmed and lashed out, splashing and struggling, kicking and fighting for breath. But the band of steel clamped around her middle was impossible to shift.

'Let me go,' she gasped, her heart thundering as whoever it was trapping her in a vice began towing her towards the side.

'Keep still,' murmured a deep masculine voice in her ear in faintly accented English. 'I've got you.'

But she hadn't needed getting. She'd been *fine*. 'Release me this instant,' she panted, shivering and breathless and scrabbling frantically to get free.

'Stop struggling. You're making things worse.'

'*I'm* making things worse?'

'I'm trying to save you from drowning.'

'I wasn't drowning.'

'You're lucky I arrived when I did.'

Lucky? Hah! 'Let. Me. Go.'

With a grind of her teeth, Willow pummelled at his forearm, but to her outrage and continued alarm the mule-headed dolt ignored her.

He didn't relax his grip on her even an inch, no matter how hard she tried to jab an elbow into his side or kick a heel into his groin. In fact, his arm seemed to *tighten*, ironically stealing the breath from her lungs in a way that inhaling water hadn't.

But perhaps he had a point about the thrashing around. It was achieving nothing other than a sapping of energy that she'd be better off saving for dry land. If she temporarily yielded to his superior physical strength and let him get on with this wholly unnecessary rescue mission of his it would be over infinitely more quickly and that could only be good.

Ceding to logic and giving up the fight for the sake of her strength and her sanity, Willow let herself go limp against him and almost instantly received a growly 'That's better' in response.

But as he carried her along with what felt like broad, confident strokes she wasn't sure that it was. Breathing might be becoming easier, but it was beginning to occur to her that she'd never been this up close and personal to a man before. At least, not moulded to one back to front as she was now.

Obviously she'd been kissed—she was twenty-four, after all—but that was as far she'd ever gone. With her condition, sex could be excruciating she'd read, and quite frankly, she had enough pain in her life without choosing to suffer further. Not only did the thought of it terrify her, she also feared things becoming awkward and having to explain. She dreaded being ridiculed, pitied, called uptight and frigid. And despite the kissing—some of which had been very nice—she'd never met anyone for whom she wanted to make that sacrifice and take that risk.

But were all chests this hard? All forearms this unforgiving? Because he'd altered his hold on her, her bottom was no longer bumping up against him, thank goodness, but now, with her head resting on his shoulder and his breath fanning her face, she was sort of lying on him—a man she didn't know and hadn't even seen—and it was unsettling to say the least.

To her relief, they reached the edge of the pool within moments. The minute the band of steel around her waist loosened, Willow bobbed away and grabbed onto the side. Taking a deep breath to calm herself, she swiped the water from her eyes then turned to face her supposed rescuer, fully prepared to demand to know who he was and what he thought he was doing.

But at the sight of him the words dried up

on her tongue. Her pulse skipped a beat and her lungs constricted all over again. He had eyes the colour of raw umber, olive skin that was testament to his Greek heritage and a bone structure that would have made Michelangelo weep. His dark hair was plastered to his head, but she knew from the photos she'd been shown it was lamp-black and ochre streaked. He was very handsome and very stern. Exactly as his mother had described.

And as she recalled Selene's myriad complaints about her eldest son, the tales of control and power he apparently liked to wield over her whenever the opportunity arose and the frequent comments about how much he'd disapprove of the portrait if he knew of its existence, all Willow could think as her heart beat a fraction faster than normal and wariness wound through her, was: What fun was he planning to spoil here?

While an obviously simmering Willow turned to paddle towards the steps, Leo shook the water from his hair then hauled himself out of the pool in one powerful move, still recovering from the events of the past five minutes.

He'd arrived at the villa in one of Athens's most exclusive and expensive suburbs a quarter of an hour ago, burning up with the frustration that came with his failure to date to fulfil his promise to his sister. The moment Daphne had left his office yesterday afternoon he'd swung into action. But the director of the Tate Modern had not responded as he'd expected to his demand the exhibition be cancelled and, unsurprisingly, neither Lazlo nor his mother were taking his calls. Appealing directly to the artist herself had been his only remaining option, which was why he'd commandeered the family jet and flown over from London this morning.

Having located Selene in the drawing room and furnished her with the reason for his visit, he'd ascertained Willow's whereabouts, then stalked the length of the space and out onto the terrace. A flash of movement had had him heading for the pool. En route, he'd clocked a book and a long drink on the table beside the lounger over which a towel lay draped, and had cynically thought that in the month she'd been here allegedly working, his mother's portraitist had made herself extremely comfortable at the luxurious, fully staffed villa.

Briefly, he'd wondered whether the offer he'd put together to get rid of her and the picture would be enough or whether she'd spot an opportunity and force him to double it. But then he'd seen her suddenly stop midlength, thrash about and sink beneath the surface of the water, and the innate instinct to save someone in trouble had overridden any suspicion about what she was and what she might be up to.

Leo didn't regret his actions in the slightest, however much Willow had protested she hadn't needed his help. He might be ruthless in business and intent on neutralising the threat she posed to Daphne's happiness, but he drew the line at letting her drown in order to achieve that goal. And thanks to a swimming gala years ago, during which his youngest sister, Olympia, had fainted in the pool and no one but him had noticed her sink to the bottom, he knew that it was better to be safe than sorry.

What he *did* regret however, was that he was now dripping wet and bereft of the shoes he'd toed off and the jacket he'd stripped from his torso in his haste to dive in to the rescue. With his shirt plastered to his chest and his trousers clinging to his thighs, the image he currently presented was about as far from the cool control and unassailable authority he preferred to exude as it was possible to get.

But at least he had height and breadth in his favour, he thought grimly, as he pulled off his socks and bent to pick up his jacket. Clamped to his chest as he'd carried her to safety, Willow had felt considerably smaller than him. Somehow delicate, despite the kicking. And, once she'd finally relaxed against him, very supple and very soft.

Not that her body was of any interest to him, of course. Her curves, which were barely contained by the tiny black bikini she wore, were generous and her legs were tanned and shapely, but he'd never been distracted by a woman and he wasn't about to be now. He wasn't his mother, after all, ruled by whim, by emotion, by carnality. He wasn't self-centred and thoughtless, scandalous and embarrassing.

Not these days, at least.

As a youth, he'd lived a pretty hedonistic and carefree existence, taking for granted his family's wealth and privilege that meant he could pursue his love of sailing with the best boats and finest kit, and believing himself invincible. But ever since his father's fatal heart attack, which had catapulted him sooner than anyone had anticipated into the role he'd been destined to fill—for which he had not been ready—he'd been a model of strength and restraint. These days, he was focused and driven. With the occasional exception that generally involved obstreperous family members, he was used to being obeyed. He was accustomed to having his demands carried out and he got results.

So he didn't think it a disappointment when Willow towelled herself off and slipped on a silky pink robe that hid her body from view. He easily wiped from his memory the feel of her bottom bumping up against him as he'd towed her to the side and the satiny softness of her skin beneath his fingers. He had no further reason to find himself so close to her that he could make out flecks of amber in the emerald-green depths of her eyes. Her toenails— each painted a different colour—offended his need for order, so he simply wouldn't look at them, and that went for the many earrings and the twinkling nose stud she wore, too.

The only thing that mattered was that he accomplished his mission to ensure his sister's wedding went off without a hitch. And that he would do, right here, right now, whatever it took.

Had Willow not been busy contemplating the reason Leo Stanhope was paying his mother a visit and somehow sensing that it couldn't be good, she'd have thought it a crying shame he donned his jacket and fastened the buttons because his shirt, rendered transparent by his dip in the pool, showcased muscles that really were something else.

However, who or what he looked like was as irrelevant as his impressive size and the raw physicality that had been in such evidence only a moment ago. If by some unfortunate chance he'd found out about the portrait and was here to express his displeasure, she needed to keep her wits about her. If he wasn't, if he'd just happened to catch sight of her flailing about through the window and simply hadn't fancied the paperwork of a hypothetical drowning, then all she needed to do was introduce herself, muster up a grudging 'thank you' and get back to work. Either way—and the latter was infinitely preferable, of course—polite professionalism was the way forward, she was sure.

'Willow Jacobs,' she said, holding out her hand and bestowing upon him her widest smile. 'You must be Leo.'

With a quick frown, he gave her hand a perfunctory shake then strode past her and pulled out one of the six chairs that surrounded the poolside table.

'I know who you are,' he said flatly, pointing at the seat with one long tanned finger. 'Sit down. We need to talk.'

Willow dropped her hand and her stomach sank. Right. So he *was* here for her. 'About?'

'Your portrait of my mother naked.'

As she'd feared.

The set of Leo's expression and the severity of his tone suggested he'd brook no argument, and from what Selene had told her, he was used to ordering about people who immediately rushed to do his bidding, but that was just tough. Willow had no intention of being one of them. Certainly not if he was here to scupper the future she so badly needed. There was simply too much at stake.

And besides, he might be standing there all darkly forbidding and smoulderingly intense, the sun setting behind him giving him a god-like glow, but thanks to Selene and her stories, she knew that that he wasn't as invincible as he obviously liked to make out.

'I prefer to stand,' she said, lifting her chin and folding her arms across her chest to reinforce the message that she was not going to be intimidated.

'Fine.' He stalked towards her and came to a halt a couple of feet in front of her. 'I'll get straight to the point,' he said, close enough for her to be able to feel the simmering tension vibrating off him, close enough to touch.

Willow ignored the instinct to take a step back out of his powerful orbit and stood her ground. 'Please do.'

'This painting of yours will not be going on display.'

What? 'That is not your decision to make.'

His jaw tightened. 'It must never see the light of day.'

'It absolutely must,' she said, straightening her spine and lifting her chin a tiny bit higher. 'It's an exceptional piece. My best work yet.'

'That's irrelevant.'

Willow bristled. However handsome and well-constructed he was, his presumption was staggering. 'Not to me.'

'I'll double what my mother's paying you.'

'No.'

'I'll triple it.'

'No.'

'How much do you want?'

'I'm not for bribing,' she said with a bluntness that matched his own.

He arched one sceptical eyebrow. 'I find that hard to believe.'

For a moment, she just stared at him in appalled horror. Was he implying what she thought he was implying? 'And what, exactly, is that supposed to mean?'

'You're hardly a well-known name,' he said, and she inwardly winced because it was undeniably true. 'So how did you come to be painting my mother?'

'Not that it's any of your business,' said Willow icily, 'but we met at the launch of a new art gallery in London. I was waitressing. She admired my hair. We got chatting. She mentioned wanting a portrait done. I sent her some photos of my work and that was it.'

'Does it always take a month?'

'Two to three weeks, usually.' To fit around her menstrual cycle, not that she was going to tell him *that*. 'Hers took longer because she kept disappearing.'

'So you moved in.'

'She invited me to,' she said, annoyed that she was even bothering to give him an explanation when none was needed. 'She was really quite insistent about it. I got the impression she was lonely.'

'Lonely?' he said with a bark of humourless laughter. 'That's ridiculous. She's constantly surrounded by people, some of whom have been known to take advantage of her ridiculous generosity.'

'Yes, well, someone once sang about being alone in a crowded room, and you can think what you like about people taking advantage of your mother, but I'm not one of them.'

Leo's dark eyes narrowed while he considered her words and despite the outrage swirling around inside her, Willow grudgingly supposed she could see where his concern was coming from even if she didn't appreciate his accusations. His family was not only one of the most glamorous in the world, it was also one of the wealthiest. He regularly appeared on various rich lists. He didn't know anything about her, and, possibly understandably, he obviously didn't trust Selene to make sensible decisions.

'What's your objection to the portrait anyway?' she said, choosing to let the matter of her motives go because either he believed her or he didn't, and bringing the conversation back to the point. 'Have you actually seen it?'

Leo visibly shuddered and winced. 'What? No. I can't think of anything worse.'

'You should. It's very tasteful. Your mother is beautiful. She's a woman in love and that shines through.'

'She's always in love. Or thinks she is.'

The disdain evident in his voice piqued her curiosity. 'Do you have a problem with love?'

His jaw tightened. 'I have a problem with

a life-size nude picture of my middle-aged mother going on public display.'

'You don't know how lucky you are to have a middle-aged mother to be captured on paper and put on display in the first place,' she said, swallowing down the small tight lump that lodged in her throat. 'Mine died a decade ago, when she was thirty-nine and I was fourteen. I'd give anything to have her back and paint her now, clothed or unclothed, whatever her behaviour.'

Some undefinable emotion flickered across Leo's expression, but thankfully he didn't produce the standard yet meaningless, in this context, *I'm sorry*.

'Tell me what you want, Miss Jacobs,' he said instead, which at least had the benefit of yanking her out of her melancholy and refocusing her thoughts. 'There will be something.'

His arrogance was outrageous, but Willow was not to be deterred. No amount of money— or anything else—was going to sway her. Not when everything she'd ever dreamed of professionally was within touching distance.

'Mr Stanhope,' she said with a tight smile. 'Leo, if I may. It's not about the money. At least, not entirely. It's more about opportunity, and this exhibition is a once-in-a-lifetime one.

I want my name to be on everyone's lips in the art world. I want to be the go-to artist for a portrait in pastel. I've waited a long time for this break. So you could offer me the sun, the moon and the stars and it would be in vain. There is absolutely nothing you can say or do that will make me change my mind.'

'No?' he said after a beat. 'Well, how about this? The picture is due to go on show two weeks on Monday, right?'

Wondering where he was going with this, Willow nodded warily. 'That's correct.'

'My sister is getting married the following Thursday.'

'I heard.' Selene had shown her the dress she was planning to wear. Willow had only just about managed to hide her appal and keep to herself her thoughts about the mother of the bride wearing white—and not all that much of it—to her daughter's special day.

'The fact that a wedding is even taking place is a miracle,' said Leo. 'When Daphne was thirteen she was diagnosed with leukaemia. The outlook was not good. She wasn't expected to live more than five years. But she has. She's in remission. And now she's found someone with whom she wants to spend the rest of her hopefully long life. This wedding of hers is a huge event. A celebration of survival as well as their relationship. There will be seven hundred guests in attendance. Family. Friends. Europe's elite and its biggest gossips. I will not have Daphne, or her fiancé, being upstaged by anything or anyone. Least of all a scandalous portrait of our thoughtless, self-centred, hedonistic mother.'

Leo stopped, a muscle pounding in his cheek, his dark eyes blazing, as if this mattered a lot to him, as if it wasn't really about the picture at all. And as Willow processed his words and the tone in which they'd been delivered, which suggested he cared about his sister deeply and wasn't simply out to spoil anyone's fun, she realised she'd been wrong. Because there *was* something that could change her mind, after all.

CHAPTER TWO

LEO WAITED FOR Willow's response to his last line of defence, his heart beating oddly fast and his head pounding. Persuading her to see the situation his way was proving harder than he'd anticipated. In his experience, the other side always, *always* capitulated. But not the woman standing in front of him with her arms folded across her chest and her chin up. Disconcertingly, she didn't seem remotely fazed by him.

Once he'd realised she wasn't motivated by money, all that had remained was revealing the truth about the situation and appealing to her better nature, but if that didn't work he didn't know what he'd do. Steal the portrait and then destroy it?

He was finding it hard to think straight. His attention kept being drawn to those damn multicoloured toenails. He thought he could make out a faint hint of pink in her still damp hair, which was absurd. The gem in her nostril kept catching the light of the setting sun. And how many piercings did one pair of ears actually need?

Something about this woman was making him feel unhinged. His stomach was roiling in a way that even the choppiest waters he'd encountered while competitively sailing hadn't managed. He had the unpleasant feeling that she could unravel his control with a click of her fingers if he didn't exercise extreme caution, which was a concern because without it, he suspected the many plates he had spinning could well crash to the ground.

But *why* was she having this effect on him? He'd faced down heads of governments. The toughest of business figures. His mother. This bizarre…susceptibility…was as nonsensical as it was unacceptable.

'All right,' she eventually said, snapping him out of his disturbing thoughts and back to the conversation. 'I suggest a compromise.'

He blinked, astonishment jolting through him. 'A compromise?'

'Is that not a word you're familiar with?' she asked dryly.

'No.'

'Then allow me to explain. The portrait is too good and too important to me to be hidden away gathering dust. So it *will* go on display somewhere soon, and that's non-negotiable. But I can understand your concerns with regard to the gossip about your mother overshadowing your sister's big day. So I'm prepared to agree to a delay.'

A delay?

'On one condition.'

'Which is?'

'I'd like an invitation to the wedding reception.'

Outwardly, Leo didn't move a muscle. Inwardly, he reeled. That was ballsy of her. But why was he even entertaining this conversation when he could simply ransack the house for the portrait and cart it off with him? Where were his wits? Why were his feet glued to the ground instead of carrying him to the house to do just that?

'The exhibition is a temporary one,' she continued in the same confident tone before he could issue a flat out no. 'By the time the wedding's over it will be, too. I'll miss my best chance of establishing my career. But if your guests are as influential as you claim, then access to them will make up for it. I promise to be subtle. I won't hand out cards or do anything crass like that. You won't even notice I'm there.

One more guest among hundreds isn't a huge price to pay to secure your sister's happiness, surely. But it's entirely up to you.'

She stopped, looking as cool as the proverbial cucumber, and he realised with an unsettling jolt that she'd turned the tables on him. He'd set out intending to bribe her into submission if necessary, but she was now the one who had him over a barrel, because he couldn't steal the portrait and destroy it. She—or more likely, his mother—would probably have him arrested for theft and criminal damage, which would create an even greater scandal. If he wasn't feeling so on edge and off balance, he'd have been impressed by Willow's swift thinking and sharp practice.

'So do we have a deal?'

Absolutely not, was the answer Leo instinctively wanted to give. *He* proposed deals. He led the charge. He rarely surrendered control, especially not to beautiful but truculent women with multicoloured toenails, too many piercings and possibly pink hair.

And yet, as he recalled his intention to achieve his goal right here, right now, whatever it took, he had to reassess. 'Whatever it took' was turning out to be remarkably little. He'd been prepared to shell out thousands. All

Willow and her better nature wanted was an invitation to a party which, as she'd so astutely pointed out, was going to be attended by hundreds anyway. If he agreed to her demands, he'd actually be getting off exceedingly lightly.

His sister's happiness was more than worth the minor temporary cession of the control he valued so highly. It was worth everything, so he gave a short nod, a tight smile and said, 'We have a deal.'

It had taken Willow twenty-four hours to get over the poolside encounter with Leo. Having sealed the deal with a bone-crushing handshake and a grudging request for her email address, he'd snatched up his shoes and socks and stalked off, leaving her scarcely able to believe she'd had the nerve to do what she'd done.

It could so easily have gone the other way. If he'd refused the invitation point-blank then that would have been that. She was ambitious, sure, but she wasn't so ruthless she'd ride roughshod over another woman's happiness. Especially one who'd suffered so much with her health, which she knew a little about. She'd have delayed the exhibition of the portrait anyway and her career would have been set back by who knew how much, but she'd have found solace in knowing she'd done the right thing.

However, he hadn't refused, thank God. Her gamble had paid off. The question now was, would this one?

The taxi that had picked her up from the hostel she'd moved to after finishing the portrait last week drew up to the kerb some distance from the entrance to Athens's finest hotel. At the sight of the guests making their way up the steps to the front door, the nerves knotting Willow's stomach tightened. Camera flashes were going off left, right and centre, illuminating the dusk and making her blink, and for one brief moment she wondered what on earth she'd been thinking. This was the social event of the year. Celebrities, royalty, the great and the good, and...*her*?

Was she mad?

This wasn't her world. She wasn't wearing a ten-thousand-euro outfit and half a ton of diamonds. Her dress was plain and simple and borrowed, couriered over by a friend back home who owned a shop that rented out evening wear. She wore no jewellery apart from the gold watch she'd inherited from her mother, the tiny diamond in her nose that she'd bought with the money she'd earned from her first-ever commission and a variety of studs and rings that adorned her ears just because she liked them.

But then she rallied. The evening ahead wasn't one to enjoy. It was work. She had a plan, a future to secure and the stakes were high. She was no better or worse than any of the other guests and she could talk to anyone. She hoped. So there'd be no more nerves. No more doubt about her place at this party. Her chin would be up and her shoulders back.

She wasn't remotely bothered about crossing paths with the brother of the bride and host of the reception. Leo, with his wet-shirt-clad chest and his admirable concern for his sister, had occupied far too much of her head space over the last couple of weeks—even when she'd been confined to her hostel for a few days, curled up on the bed in agony and popping painkillers like sweets—but she didn't intend to seek him out. There was no need to do so and it was highly unlikely he'd relish the opportunity to talk to her anyway, given the manner in which she'd wheedled her invitation out of him.

No. She would not be distracted by anyone or anything this evening. She would not dwell on the fact that night after night she'd woken up hot and achy and shaking after dreaming of him, which was baffling when their one and only encounter had been so brief and hostile. She would stop wondering whether he could truly be as devastatingly handsome as she recalled. She would put him entirely from her mind. If their eyes did happen to meet across a crowded room and she discovered that he *was* as gorgeous as she remembered, she'd offer him a cool smile of acknowledgement and that would be it.

She'd created a golden opportunity for herself and her career here, she reminded herself firmly as she took a deep breath, adjusted her dress and opened the door. A chance to generate work and build her reputation like no other. And she was not going to waste it.

'So far, so good.'

In response to the dry comment in Greek that came from his left, Leo swung his gaze away from the guests beginning to amass in the hall below and rested it on his brother, the next one down in age.

Zander was right. So far, things had been very good. Way better than he'd anticipated, in fact. The ceremony that had taken place this morning at the Metropolitan Cathedral of Athens had gone off without a hitch. The dozen or so knee-high bridesmaids had behaved beautifully. The bride had looked radiant as he'd led her down the aisle, and the groom—ridiculously overcome by emotion—had even shed a tear when he'd said his vows. Selene had ditched the white in favour of an unexpectedly age-and occasion-appropriate pale blue skirt and matching jacket and had exhibited far more restraint than Leo could ever have hoped.

Yet he couldn't relax.

The minute he'd woken up this morning his gut had started to churn with apprehension and adrenalin, a leaden weight settling in his chest. Despite the success of the day, none of that had eased. He had to remain alert. He had to keep an eye on his mother because he knew from experience that when it came to her, things could turn on a sixpence.

'The night is young,' he muttered as he resumed his perusal of the throng at the centre of which were his sister and brand-new brother-in-law, looking absurdly happy, as if the car crash of her parents' marriage hadn't given them even the tiniest pause for thought. 'There's still plenty of opportunity for Selene to make a scene.'

'She hasn't yet,' Zander pointed out, 'and I'm assured she won't.'

'Who by?'

'Atticus told Olympia who told Thalia who told me that apparently the woman who was painting her had a word.'

At the eventual reference to Willow, every one of Leo's senses sharpened and his entire body seemed to vibrate, as if he'd suddenly been plugged in and switched on. If someone had asked him to recite the order of siblings through which the information had travelled he'd have failed. 'What sort of a word?'

'A subtle one, apparently.'

'Well, that won't last long,' he muttered. 'We all know subtle doesn't work.'

'Seems to be working so far,' Zander said. 'Who'd have thought? A random artist who's known her for approximately two months succeeds where the rest of us, who've known her for years, fail. She must be quite something.'

She was. Although Leo had no idea quite what.

'You met her, didn't you?'

Met her. Dived into a pool to save her. Argued with her, bargained with her and dreamed about her ever since… 'I did.'

'What was her name?'

'Willow Jacobs.'

Saying the words out loud made his blood

heat and his skin prickle, but that reaction was nothing new when it came to her. He'd been driven to distraction by the woman over the last couple of weeks. That their encounter had lasted no more than half an hour and had hardly been scintillating didn't matter. Try as he might, he hadn't been able to get the image of her—arms folded, chin up, green eyes lit with cool fire—out of his head.

In his dreams, she didn't don a robe on exiting the pool. No. That would be far too considerate. Instead, she sidled up to him, all glorious curves and sultry smiles, while he remained rooted to the spot. She pushed aside the lapels of his jacket, put her hands to the buttons of his sodden shirt and huskily said something along the lines of 'Why don't we get out of these wet things?' He, seeing this as an excellent idea rather than a cringe-worthy cliché, then invariably pulled her into his arms and lowered her to a lounger before setting about doing as she suggested.

'What's she like?'

Gorgeous. Annoying. Disturbing. 'I don't know,' he muttered. 'Our encounter was brief.'

And that was what was so irritating about the bizarrely intense effect she'd had on him. He didn't know her. He didn't particularly like her. She had zero respect for his authority. She challenged the order and control he valued so highly and ultimately she'd blackmailed him.

Yet he could recall every word of their conversation, every arch of her eyebrow and every jut of her chin. He wanted to know what she felt and tasted like. The sounds she'd make as he ran his hands and mouth over her and then finally sank into her. What was even more unnerving but equally baffling, he couldn't stop thinking about the fleeting sadness that had filled her expression when she'd mentioned her mother and pondering the nature of their relationship.

Willow—a woman with multiple piercings, a slapdash attitude towards nail varnish and possibly pink hair, whose nanosecond of vulnerability seemed to be permanently etched into his head and who was the complete opposite of the cool, polished, one-earring-per-ear type he usually went for—was immensely distracting on a number of levels, and it was frustrating in the extreme.

'Daph said you invited her tonight.'

Schooling his features so that not a hint of his inner turmoil showed, Leo shoved his hands in his pockets and gave a casual shrug. 'All part of the package to keep the wedding scandal-free.'

'So where is she?'

'No idea.'

Whether she came tonight or not, he didn't care. She wasn't the cause of the adrenalin that had been pounding through him since this morning and he wasn't scanning the guests for her now. He was standing on the balcony simply to get some breathing space after a hectic day. That he had a view of the gathering throng was merely an unintended consequence of that. He wasn't watching the door. He had eyes on his mother and that was where they'd stay.

Yet even before his brother blew out a breath and murmured a low, admiring 'Wow', Leo registered the moment Willow arrived. His entire body tensed. His clothes suddenly felt too tight. His heart rate accelerated and he was aware of it drumming fast and hard everywhere.

'Who's that?'

Despite his every intention not to, he shifted slightly to look in the direction of Zander's gaze, at the woman who was turning to the waiter standing at the door with a tray upon which stood a dozen glasses of champagne. In direct opposition to every effort he made to remain immune, the impact of her hit him like a kick in the chest.

He recognised the wide, stunning smile she

gave the waiter as she accepted a glass. He could entirely sympathise with the poor guy, who was blushing and staring at her like a deer in the headlights. That smile had knocked him for six the first time he'd seen it, too.

On the other hand, maybe it was the dress—long, pale yellow, sequinned and just tight enough—that had rendered the waiter speechless. Or her hair. What colour *was* it? Or should that be colours? Because it wasn't just pink, as he assumed when it had been wet from the pool. The wavy predominantly blond tresses that were swept off her face and rippled down her back were also streaked with blue and green. She didn't just paint in pastels…she wore them on her head.

'That's the artist,' he said, running a finger around the inside of his collar and stretching his neck to ease his oddly laboured breathing.

'A unicorn appears to be missing its mane.'

'So it would seem.'

'Want to bet that she's the only one here with beads in her hair?'

'No.'

'She's stunning.'

'If you like that sort of thing.' Which, to his irritation, apparently, he did, despite the offensive nature of pretty much everything about her.

While Zander continued to mutter appreciative inanities about Willow's singular look, in raptures over her striking features and spectacular figure, Leo watched her enter the mêlée and introduce herself to a group of Italian socialites. As she chatted and laughed he thought darkly that it was no wonder she didn't need business cards. She was unforgettable. Anything but subtle. And as for not noticing her, how on earth would *that* ever be possible?

As if aware he was watching her, she suddenly glanced up, her eyes locking with his. For a second she went still, then flashed him another of those incendiary smiles, which momentarily stole the breath from his lungs and fogged his head.

But he recovered swiftly enough. He was well accustomed to stamping out rogue flares of wildness that he'd occasionally experienced over the years when his guard slipped. So he offered her a brief nod—no smile—in return, switched his attention back to his mother, and they were done. His and Willow's paths need never cross again. He had no reason to talk to her. No need to thank her for persuading Selene to see sense for once. He would not surrender to the demands of his body, however clamouring they were, and seek her out simply because he wanted to. He would not be that weak.

'She has quite a smile.'

She did. 'I hadn't noticed.'

'No, well, lucky for me, she's my type, not yours.'

Once again, Zander was right. And that was fine. His brother could make Willow's acquaintance and flirt with her all he liked. He wasn't remotely bothered. It wasn't as if she'd be around for long. The women his brother set his sights on never were. 'Good luck.'

'Thanks. Not that I'll need it. You should try it some time.'

'Try what?'

'Lightening up. You know what they say about all work and no play.'

Leo stiffened. Yes, well, *someone* had to keep the multibillion business he'd inherited from their father afloat. 'You play enough for both of us.'

'Only because you won't let go of the reins and I have a lot of spare time to fill.'

'You're chief commercial officer.'

'Which, thanks to your control issues, I do with one hand tied behind my back.'

Leo didn't have the head space for his brother's familiar grumblings. He'd turned his mind to strategising. Tomorrow he'd have a nice little chat with his mother and make her see the error of her ways in wanting to put the portrait on show. How he'd forgotten that he held her purse strings and therefore all the cards was a mystery. Within twenty-four hours, scandal would be averted. Willow and the havoc she wreaked on him would be gone and the compromise she'd negotiated out of him would be history. Once he'd stopped dreaming about her, he could forget he'd ever met her. Order would be restored and normality would resume.

In the meantime, there was an evening to get through, an unpredictable parent to keep an eye on and seven hundred guests to greet.

'Where are you going?' Zander murmured, not even bothering to take his gaze off the unicorn mermaid siren down below.

'The net worth of this room runs into the hundreds of billions,' said Leo, the irrational and inexplicable irritation he suddenly felt towards his brother as unnecessary as it was perplexing. 'There's business to be done. You and I, therefore, are going to mingle.'

The first thing that had taken Willow's breath away the moment she'd entered the hall was the enormous sparkling chandelier that looked

suitable for high jinks of the glamorous socialite kind. The second was the sheer splendour
of the space—the lavishly painted ceiling, the
old masters on the walls, the marble, the gilt,
the silk. Shortly after that, it was Leo.

Fortified by half a glass of bone-dry champagne, she'd been enjoying the conversation
she'd been having with two Milanese countesses and one Puglian landowner while dis-
creetly jotting down their names and email
addresses in the small notebook she'd stashed
in the hidden pocket of her dress.

But then, quite suddenly, she'd tensed. A
shiver had raced down her spine and her skin
had broken out in goose bumps. She'd glanced
up and around and a second later her eyes had
locked with Leo's, as if his were a magnet and
hers iron filings. She'd managed to muster up
a smile in acknowledgement, as planned, but,
very much *not* as planned, she'd been so rocked
by the immediate impact of his smouldering
good looks that she'd lost track of the conversation.

Fortunately for her dignity, Leo had then disappeared from view. Willow had snapped out
of her trance and recalled what she was meant
to be doing, which was ignoring distractions
and working the room.

Dinner had been delicious, her table companions interesting and engaging and, happily, very keen on having themselves committed to paper. Leo's speech, which had switched seamlessly between Greek, English, French, Spanish and Italian had been loudly and enthusiastically applauded. She hadn't understood much more than a quarter of what he said, but that might have been because, despite her best efforts to prevent it, all she could really focus on was his mouth and the way it moved.

Now she'd been persuaded to the dance floor by his brother, who apparently had been up on the balcony with Leo earlier, not that she'd noticed. He was handsome and charming but in a hard, hollow kind of a way that left her strangely unmoved even though over coffee and chocolates he'd made her laugh until her sides ached.

'How about we take this somewhere more private?' Zander murmured in her ear as he drew her closer and continued to manoeuvre her skilfully around the floor.

At the sensual promise she could hear in his voice, nerves fluttered in her stomach and alarm skittered through her. Flirting was one thing—and she enjoyed that as much as anyone—but she'd never taken anything anywhere and didn't particularly want to now. She was way out of her depth. She had no idea how to handle a man like Zander. He oozed experience and sexuality. All she had was honesty, which would just have to do, so she put her hands on his chest to stop any further advance and said rather abruptly, 'No, thanks.'

In response, Zander jerked back, and his eyebrows shot up in a way that suggested arrogance ran in the family. 'Seriously?'

'Sorry.'

'No need to apologise.'

'Quite right,' said a deep voice behind her, a voice that brought back the memory of being clamped against him as he towed her to the side of the pool, a voice that had murmured not so sweet nothings in her ear in her dreams night after night and now sent shivers down her spine. 'Zander, I heard the Duke of Clervaux is unhappy with his current banking provision and is seeking a change.'

Zander must have felt the tremor that ran through her for she caught a spark of curiosity in his gaze as he shifted it from her to the man standing behind her and then back again.

'Is he?' he said with a wry arch of an eyebrow.

'Yes.'

'Well, why didn't you say?' he said, releasing her and taking a step back, hands open and up. 'The lovely Willow is all yours.'

'Actually,' said Willow, not really understanding the undercurrents swirling between them but instinctively feeling the need to remind both men of her existence, lovely or not. 'I'm not anyone's.'

'Interesting,' said Zander with a grin, and off he sauntered.

CHAPTER THREE

WHAT IN THE name of Zeus was he doing? Leo wondered, his blood thrumming like an outboard motor as his brother disappeared from sight and Willow slowly turned to face him. Why was he standing in the middle of a crowded dance floor in front of a woman he'd had no intention of ever talking to again?

Over the course of the evening he'd caught regular glimpses of her, and her name had kept coming up in conversation, but he hadn't responded. He'd merely averted his gaze and changed topic. Sheer willpower had prevented him from reacting to the discovery that her dress was backless and she couldn't therefore be wearing a bra. Years of experience at containing his emotions had kept a lid on the simmering desire that threatened to boil over and consume him. But all that resolve, all that strength of character had evaporated at the sight of Willow in his brother's arms.

So much for not being bothered. One brief glance in her direction, then another when what he was witnessing sank in, and the words *hell no* had flashed through his head in bright green neon. A strange sort of red mist had descended and the urgent need to put a stop to the proceedings had flared into life. Instinct had kicked in and obliterated the cool consideration and calm objectivity with which he usually acted.

He could barely recall excusing himself from the people he'd been talking to. How many apologies had he had to mutter as he'd stalked across the dance floor? How much interest had he attracted? Why did he not care?

Whatever was going on, whatever had driven him to challenge the situation, here he was now. In front of her. Unanchored. Adrift in uncharted waters and standing beneath a giant glitter ball like an idiot with no clue how to proceed. For the first time in his life.

'Did you want something?' Willow asked with admirable composure, although the faint flush on her cheeks and the fluttering pulse at the base of her neck suggested she was anything but composed.

Her. He wanted her. And there was no rhyme

or reason to it. Just unfathomable yet clamouring need that he was struggling to subdue and a thrilling rush of adrenalin he hadn't felt since scything through the waves at twenty knots and a forty-five-degree angle over a decade ago. 'Dance with me.'

She looked him, her darkening gaze dipping to his mouth and lingering, as if she'd imagined kissing him as much as he'd imagined kissing her. After a beat, she gave a nod, a faint smile and then, to his unaccountable relief, said a little breathlessly, 'All right.'

Agreeing to dance with Leo had been a mistake.

Willow realised this the instant he wrapped one of his large warm hands around hers and planted the other on her bare back and she nearly went up in flames. Contact with his brother had left her unmoved. Contact with him was electric. Why? She had no idea.

She should have said no to his demand that she dance and walked away. Their one and only encounter had hardly been cordial. No doubt he wanted to discuss the portrait's future with her now the wedding was over and any further delay was unnecessary, and she'd moved on. She shouldn't have succumbed to curiosity.

She didn't need to know whether her dreams in any way represented reality. She was here to network and that was all that mattered.

Yet when he pulled her close she did nothing to stop him. On the contrary, she met him more than halfway. She'd never believed that magnetism between people could actually exist but here she was, pressed up against him, one hand on his shoulder, the other clasped in his. They were touching everywhere from chest to hip, and wild horses couldn't have dragged her away.

'How have you been?' he said, his voice low and gravelly as he began to slowly move her around the tight space they occupied, hemmed in by others lured by the hits Europe's number one girl band was banging out.

'Fine,' she replied, strangely husky. 'You?'

'Busy.'

'How was the ceremony?'

'Uneventful.'

'That must have been a relief.'

'You have no idea.'

His gaze roamed over her hair and her face before settling on her mouth, which instantly dried while her pulse raced. He was so close all she'd have to do was lift herself onto her toes, lean forwards an inch while exerting pressure on his shoulder to draw him down and then she'd finally know what it would be like to kiss him.

'Lovely party,' she said, battling back the temptation to do exactly that since it would be wildly inappropriate and no doubt cause a scandal he certainly wouldn't welcome.

'Hmm.'

'Dinner was delicious. Your brother is charming.'

Leo's hand tightened around hers and a quick frown creased his forehead, but only for an instant. 'That's why he's in charge of drumming up new business.'

'I imagine he's very good at it.'

'He is. As are you.'

Willow's heart thudded. Had he been watching her in action? For some reason, the thought of his eyes on her as she worked the room heated her blood. 'I try.'

'Everyone is talking about you.'

'At least I'm not the mother of the bride and naked in a frame.'

'A blessing indeed,' he murmured, but something in his expression made her wish she'd kept her mouth shut because not only did she have the unnerving feeling that he was somehow mentally undressing her, but also all she could think of now was how good he'd looked in a wet shirt and how much better he might look without anything on at all.

Swallowing hard to refocus, Willow reined in her imagination and determinedly sought refuge in manners. 'Thank you for my invitation.'

'I wasn't aware I had much choice in issuing it.'

'That's a fair point,' she had to acknowledge with the hint of a smile. 'I did blackmail you into it.'

'You did. But actually, if anyone's owed a thank-you, it's you.'

'For what?'

'I understand you're the one responsible for my mother's restraint today,' he said. 'And, I'm guessing, both her outfit in church and the dress she has on this evening.'

'You're welcome,' she said, a shiver of pleasure and relief rippling through her. 'Although I did wonder if I was overstepping by intervening.'

'You were.'

'Sorry.'

'Once again, you have no need to apologise. You have my gratitude. And Daphne's.' He leaned back an inch and tilted his head, his hold on her loosening a fraction. 'What's your secret?'

'There's no secret,' she said, relaxing a little now she was on safer conversational ground. 'I like to get to know my clients so I encourage them to talk while I work.'

'What about?'

'Whatever they want. Anything, really. It puts them at ease. Lowers their guard. And from my point of view, it gives me insight into their character, which adds a certain sort of magic to the painting. Some find it hard. Selene's the opposite.'

'That doesn't surprise me.'

'I merely asked her some curated questions and mentioned how much I imagined my own mother would have wanted to be around for my wedding and the sacrifices she'd have made to ensure it was all about me. I suggested that today might be Daphne's chance to shine. I know how difficult that can be sometimes.'

'Do you?'

'Yes.'

'In what way?'

In a constantly-being-thwarted-by-her-condition kind of a way, mainly. How many exams had she failed because she'd been in such agony she hadn't managed to turn up? How many arrangements with friends had she bailed on? How many jobs had she wanted to apply for only to realise she'd never be able to stay the course? Too many to recall.

But she was hardly going to go into all that. It was way too personal and even more inappropriate than kissing her reluctant host in the middle of a crowded dance floor.

'The art world is a hard one to break into,' she said, which both answered his question and was true.

'You've made a good start.'

She thought of the contact details that filled her notebook and felt a surge of pride. 'I hope so.'

'Where's the portrait now?'

'In storage at a gallery here in Athens, where it will stay until the unveiling your mother's planning.'

His jaw twitched and the frown was back. 'The unveiling?'

'That's right.'

'She's utterly shameless.'

Despite the giddy pleasure she felt at being in his embrace, Willow bristled. 'This is my work you're talking about, Leo. There's nothing shameful about any of it. Life drawing is a respected artistic tradition that's been around for millennia. I'm proud of what I do, and if your mother wants to celebrate her sexuality then that's to be applauded, too.'

Leo winced. 'She's nearly sixty.'

'So?'

'I should cut off her allowance.'

She stiffened in his arms and jerked back. 'You'd do that?' she breathed, staring up at him in shock.

'Yes, if necessary. She's a walking scandal and this time she's gone too far.'

'She loves life.'

'She's self-centred and thoughtless.'

'Perhaps, but she's also entertaining and, like you said, generous. She took a risk on me—a complete unknown—and she's the one who arranged the exhibition of the portrait. From my point of view, she's been nothing but supportive.'

Leo muttered something non-committal in response to that and then said, 'What was your mother like?'

'Maternal. Doting. Firm but fair and completely conventional.'

'You said she died when you were fourteen.'

'You have an excellent memory.'

'There's little of that afternoon I *don't* remember,' he said dryly. 'What happened?'

'She went into hospital for a routine surgery and never woke up from the anaesthetic.'

'That must have been devastating.'

In so many ways…

'My father's never really recovered,' she admitted, swallowing down the small lump in her throat that always formed when she thought of the sorrow that still ravaged him. 'He's more or less a recluse.'

'And you?'

Her? Hmm. Where to start? She'd become convinced that the fate that had befallen her mother could well befall her if she ever went under the knife. She'd witnessed first-hand, on a daily basis, the traumatic effect of her mother's death on her father. What if *she* went ahead with the operations she'd been told by doctors would alleviate the pain she suffered month in, month out and one day didn't wake up? He'd have lost a daughter as well as a wife and she couldn't bear to think how he'd cope with that.

From there she'd developed a deep-seated fear of romantic love and falling into it. The idea of history repeating itself had tormented her day and night for months. What would her demise—in whatever form it took—do to someone who loved her, such as a long-term boyfriend or husband of her own? Would *they* withdraw from life, destroyed and hollowed out by grief? Would *she*, if the situation were reversed?

The greater the love, it seemed, the greater the potential devastation and she couldn't—and wouldn't—put herself or anyone else in that position. In the end, she'd figured it was far safer not to let anyone emotionally close in the first place. Far easier to simply keep her heart locked up in a cage, throw away the key and get used to the loneliness. She wished she felt differently; she didn't want to be alone for ever, but it was what it was. At least her way, only one person had to suffer.

But all that was far too intimate to share, so perhaps it would be best to present him with the obvious.

'It took a while,' she said, remembering instead the shock and the sorrow and the many long solitary walks she'd taken to process what had happened. 'It rocked my world. I don't expect the grief will ever go away—or the anger, for that matter—but you learn to live with it.'

'That's true,' he said with a slight nod, never missing a step as he smoothly moved her around the dance floor. 'My father died when I was nineteen. A heart attack. Also sudden.'

'Selene said. He sounded like a formidable man.'

'He was.'

'How did they meet?'

'At an embassy party in Paris. She fell for his British stiff upper lip and dashing looks. By all accounts she was dazzling, but I suspect the real attraction was the Kallis shipping company that he wanted to merge with the Stanhope bank.'

'That's cynical.'

'Or realistic. They married after a whirlwind two-month courtship. The honeymoon didn't last long. They were fundamentally too different. She was temperamental. He was cold. And obviously clueless when it came to handling her. He was perfectly capable of disciplining us, but for some reason he stuck his head in the sand with her. She ran rings around him. Her many affairs are unfortunately well documented. No wonder he had a heart attack.'

'Yes, well, maybe "handling" is the trouble,' she said a little archly. 'Maybe you should try working out and understanding where her behaviour comes from instead.'

His eyebrows lifted. 'Did I ask for your advice?'

'No, but you have it anyway and maybe you should heed it because your current methods aren't exactly working, are they?'

'I live in hope. At least I try to do something about it instead of opting for denial without a care for the effects of her antics on the family.'

'On you?'

'None of us emerged unscathed.'

His cryptic response piqued her curiosity, but the shuttering of his expression indicated it would be pointless to probe. 'Do you know she calls you the fun police?'

'I am aware of that,' he said, the muscles of his shoulders beneath her palms relaxing a fraction, which suggested he appreciated the shift in topic. 'But my youngest sister was only nine when my father died. Someone had to be the adult.'

'And that someone was you.'

'I'm the eldest. I was the head of the family suddenly. It was my duty. And not everyone's definition of fun is the same.'

Despite believing him to be wholly misguided on the subject of his mother, Willow felt a pang of sympathy. Being landed with that *and* inheriting a vast global business at the tender age of nineteen, presumably while still grieving himself, couldn't have been easy. 'She also described you as emotionally repressed and far too serious.'

'So I've heard.'

'Does it bother you?'

'Not in the slightest. If everyone went round behaving like she does, with zero respect for the rules of society, civilisation would collapse.'

That seemed like an overly dramatic assessment of the situation, but what did she know? 'You look like her.'

'There's nothing I can do about that,' he muttered. 'All I *can* do is not act like her.'

'Is that something you struggle with?'

'Absolutely not,' he replied with a sharpness that suggested the opposite, which she found unexpectedly intriguing.

'Shall I tell you what I think?'

'I'd rather you didn't.'

'Whether or not you kill a good time and whether or not you're an ice-cold robot—her words, not mine—I think you're just a man who loves his siblings and would do anything to protect them.'

His eyes bore into hers, a muscle pounding in his cheek. 'You don't know me.'

'I know more than you think.'

'Do you know how many people challenge me?'

'No.'

'None.'

'Well, that's not healthy.'

'Even fewer attempt to negotiate with me the way you did.'

'Maybe they don't have anything to lose.'

He tilted his head and regarded her thoughtfully. 'Are you even *slightly* intimidated by me?'

By the effect he had on her, she was, a bit. But by him? 'No. But I can see why people would be. With your height and breadth and your glowering sternness, you're physically imposing. You're head of a multibillion-euro business. You exude authority and power, even when dripping wet, and you're used to your every instruction being obeyed without question. But here's the thing,' she said, leaning forwards an inch and lowering her voice. 'Remember how I told you that your mother liked to talk?'

Wariness flickered across his handsome face. 'Yes.'

'She told me that as a kid you threw tantrums. You used to have nightmares that made you cry.'

His jaw tightened and a fascinating flush hit his cheekbones. 'I'm surprised she noticed.'

'She heard it from your nanny.'

'Of course she did.'

'She said that as you got older you were reckless and wild and took risks that sometimes landed you in hospital. Apparently, you once deliberately dashed a boat on the rocks.'

'She *is* chatty,' he said, a spark of irritation lighting the dark depths of his eyes.

'You don't like being talked about.'

'I do not,' he said with a minute shake of his head. 'Unlike some, I value my privacy.'

'So is it true? About the boat?'

'Yes.'

'Why would you do a thing like that?'

A fleeting shadow darted across his features, but it was gone in an instant. 'Just one of those wild things teenagers can get up to.'

Hmm. In her world a car was more likely to be taken for a joyride than a yacht. 'So what changed?'

He frowned. 'What do you mean?'

'Well, you don't go around having tantrums and crashing boats now, do you?'

'My father died and I had to grow up. Fast. It was a steep learning curve.'

'How steep?'

'I made a few mistakes,' he admitted with a faint grimace. 'In the beginning.'

'So you might be all-powerful and mighty, but you're human, too.'

'Flesh and blood, bone and sinew.'

All of which she was becoming only too aware, she realised with a skip of her pulse as silence fell. At some point during the conversation the band had stopped and a DJ had taken over. Instead of upbeat and boppy, the music oozing out of the speakers was now sultry and Latin, more suited to an earthy Copacabana club than a swanky Athens hotel.

The lights had dimmed. Sensuality wound around the dance floor, couples moving loosely and sinuously. Willow could feel the beat thudding through her. Leo had slowed the swaying they were doing right down and was holding her impossibly close. Something about the intensity and focus with which he was looking at her made her tremble with anticipation.

What was going on in that head of his? she wondered as strange thrills of excitement began to race through her. Three weeks or so ago they'd parted on very unfriendly terms, yet she wasn't getting unfriendly vibes off him now. Latent heat was simmering in his eyes, adding fuel to the flames flickering along her veins. She could feel the hardening length of him growing and pressing against her and nerves fluttered through her once again.

She really wasn't equipped for this. She'd thought she'd been out of her depth with his brother, but she'd been paddling in the shallows. Leo was far more dangerous to her than Zander could ever be. Outwardly, he was all steely control but he had an edge that ought to have her running towards the exit because she didn't know any of the rules of the game he was playing. But that didn't seem to matter. As unwise as it undoubtedly was when they, their lives and their experiences were poles apart, she wanted to play anyway.

'Do you know what I've dreamed of recently, Willow?'

The sound of her name in his mouth made her shiver. 'No.'

'You,' he murmured, his gaze hot on hers, this conversation for them alone. 'I've dreamed of you. Every night for the last three weeks. And those dreams have been anything but nightmares.'

Her heart lurched and then began to race while her blood thickened and heated. 'I've dreamed of you, too. They've been wild.'

'I haven't been able to take my eyes off you all night.'

'It's the hair.'

He shook his head. 'It's not the hair. Or the dress.'

'Then what is it?'

'Damned if I know. But my brother was right about one thing. You are lovely.'

'You're the sexiest man I've ever met,' she said a little breathlessly, his unexpected confession loosening her lips as well as her inhibitions. 'I want to draw you.'

'I have something else in mind.'

'What?'

He stared at her mouth and lowered his head, so slowly the anticipation was almost painful. His lips came down on hers and in that instant everything else—the music, the people, the party—disappeared. All Willow could focus on was the heat and skill of his mouth, his hands sliding to her hips so he could mould her better to him, and clinging on for dear life.

She wound her arms around his neck and tangled her fingers in his hair and the kiss that had started out light and teasing deepened into something darker and wilder.

Leo moved one hand to the back of her head and the other up her side to her breast, and she moaned. Instinctively, she tilted her hips and rubbed them against his in an attempt to relieve the throbbing between her legs, but the low growl that that elicited from him simply stoked her desire.

She'd never experienced need like it. She felt

crazed. Drugged. She wanted him naked. She wanted to explore his body by tracing every inch of skin, every muscle he possessed, and then she wanted him on top of her and in her. And it wouldn't be painful. It would be magnificent.

She lowered a hand to the waistband of his trousers and tugged at his shirt. He brushed her nipple with his thumb and she nearly jumped out of her skin. She was trembling with need, mindless with desire, completely ready to sink to the floor with him and take that risk she'd always feared, when suddenly, through the haze of longing, as if it came from far, far away, she heard a dry, amused voice call out, 'Hey. You two. Get a room.'

As if doused by a deluge of icy water, Leo instantly let Willow go and jerked back, shock and horror reeling through him as reality hit with the force of a sledgehammer.

What was he doing?

What the hell did he think he was *doing*?

He'd danced with her. He'd talked to her and told her things he'd never told another living soul. And then he'd *kissed* her. Right here on the dance floor, in the midst of all these people. Without Zander's timely intervention, he'd have set about stripping her naked and he doubted she'd have stopped him. She'd pulled at his shirt and moaned low in her throat, as if desperate to get her hands on his skin, as if she'd been as oblivious to their surroundings as he.

Confusion and appal rushed through him, tightening his chest and coating every inch of his skin in a cold sweat as he thought about what could so easily have happened. The scandal would have surpassed anything his mother had done. It would have shredded his image and destroyed his authority. It would have ruined him. What they *had* done was mortifying enough. Kissing and groping each other in public? He hadn't even engaged in that kind of thing as a permanently horny adolescent.

What on earth was the matter with him? At the start of the evening he'd resolved to ignore her and he rarely changed plan mid-course. But the plan had not only changed, it had blown up in his face. In response to overwhelming desire that he should have nevertheless been able to manage, his rigidly maintained composure had crumbled to dust in an instant.

Well, whatever was going on, whatever madness he'd been afflicted by, it would not happen again, he assured himself grimly as he took a step back and removed himself from Willow's dangerously bewitching orbit. He would not allow himself to be ruled by things over which he had no command. He had no time for emotions with their unpredictability and volatility, the chaos they caused and the pain they could inflict. He might look like his mother, but, as he'd told Willow, he would not act like her. He would not be that weak, that selfish.

Nor would he ever again put himself in a position in which his hard-won control came under threat. He'd never forget the moment he'd learned his father had died and realised that from that moment on he had sole responsibility for his family and the business. He could still recall the onslaught of emotions that had smashed through his weakened defences—the stunning shock, the agonising grief and then the raw, blind panic. The nauseating awareness that he was too young and too unprepared. The crippling knowledge that the shoes he was expected to step into were too big.

For days, bombarded with questions, documents to sign and decisions to make, he'd floundered, terrified that he was going to screw up and let everyone down. A month in and he'd concluded the only way he was going to be able to handle his new role was to bury the wilder side of his nature and the dizzying, unwelcome emotions that had sprung free, and knuckle down.

He'd abandoned his hopes and dreams and given up the yachts. He'd stamped out the bitter, shameful resentment that churned through him like bile because deep down he'd never asked for what he'd been given and didn't want any of it. Ruthless control would carry him through, he'd figured, and he'd spent years honing it into an impenetrable shield of stone and steel, designed to both protect himself and others and handle the immense burden he bore.

Now summoning up every drop of strength he possessed with the ease borne from experience, Leo felt the familiar blanket of ice-cold calm envelop him, which meant he could banish the events of the last quarter of an hour from his head and forget they'd ever happened. As the mad heat disappeared and reason returned, he could look at Willow's swollen mouth, her flushed cheeks and tousled hair and her eyes glazed with lingering desire and not respond at all.

'Enjoy the rest of your evening,' he said with a tight smile and a brief nod, as if she were any other guest rather than one with the potential to upturn his life and decimate everything he valued. 'Good night.'

CHAPTER FOUR

WILLOW RATHER ENVIED the self-possession and stability with which Leo spun on his heel and strode off. She'd never felt less in control of herself in her life. Her head was swimming. Her heart was pounding. It was a complete miracle that her legs were holding her up.

What a kiss…

It had been a kiss to which every other kiss she'd ever had paled in comparison. It had been passionate, all-consuming and mind-blowing. She could still feel the pressure of his mouth on hers and the hard muscles beneath her hands. The hot, heady desire that had taken over her body and turned it into nothing but sensation.

And she wanted more.

Much more.

Because finally, after all these years of anxiety and stress, disappointment and regret, she'd met a man with whom she positively *longed* to lose her virginity. There'd be no awkwardness or embarrassment or frigidity to worry about if things progressed and then went wrong because nothing *would* go wrong.

How could sex with Leo possibly hurt when he had the ability to melt her bones and turn her body to mush? He just had to look to her and she burned. His touch set her alight. And his mouth…well…it was a wicked, wonderful thing. Willow was no expert, obviously, but surely the chemistry they shared had to be off the charts. It would be glorious, fireworks and ecstasy from start to finish.

But it wasn't just the physical aspect of what they'd done and what she wanted to do that so appealed. Spending time with Selene and listening to her tales of adventure and passion had emphasised how staid and small her own life was in comparison. Adventure was hard to come by when work was haphazard and income was irregular. Romantic relationships— even love-free ones—were out of the question with the disruption her endometriosis caused and the possibility of infertility.

However, tonight she'd had a glimpse of both adventure *and* passion—until they'd been interrupted and he'd spooked, which was understandable, given where they'd been, what they'd been doing and his distaste for scandal. It had been sublime and she couldn't help thinking, what if they hadn't been heckled by Zander? Would Leo have manoeuvred her into a dark corner to continue with the kissing in private? Would he have taken things even further and given her the experience she so badly wanted?

She didn't know and quite possibly never would. His parting shot had been definitive and now, with the way he was cutting a determined path through the guests and striding towards the door with only a brief stop for a quick word with the happy couple, it looked as though he planned to leave.

With every purposeful step away from her he took, the hope and excitement whipping through her system withered that little bit more, deflating her by the second. Would she ever again meet someone like him? Someone who had such an extraordinarily intense effect on her? It didn't seem likely. Men like him didn't grow on trees.

So why was she standing here like a lemon?

Why wasn't she going after him and telling him she wanted more?

What was she *doing*?

She had nothing to lose and everything to gain from pursuing the passion she'd just experienced. Who cared if they were as different as two people could be? She wasn't after a happy-ever-after with him. She wasn't after that with *anyone*. She just wanted one night.

And if he didn't?

Well, she was tough enough to handle rejection, should it come to that. Fighting to establish a career in the notoriously tight-knit art world had strengthened her determination to go for what she wanted, and right now she wanted him and more of the excitement he'd shown her. Her mother's sudden death had proved that life was short, and she'd far rather regret something she had done than something she hadn't.

So, yielding to the instinct that was now drumming so insistently through her and blocking out the voice in her head demanding to know if she'd gone stark, raving mad, Willow galvanised into action. Because if Leo *was* leaving, then he wasn't leaving alone.

The large silver car pulled up outside the hotel just as Leo pushed through the heavy glass door and emerged into the warm Athens night. He stashed the phone he'd used to summon it in the inside pocket of his dinner jacket and jogged down the steps to the pavement. With a brief nod at Stavros, the chauffeur who was now holding open the rear door nearest the kerb, he climbed in, instantly welcoming the peace and seclusion.

The door closed with a soft *thunk*, shutting out the madness and the chaos, and relief flooded his system. He'd had such a lucky escape, he thought grimly, tugging at one end of his bow tie to loosen the knot, then undoing the top two buttons of his dress shirt and feeling as though he could breathe for the first time in hours.

Could he even begin to hope that his moment of complete and utter insanity had been witnessed by no one but his brother? It had been dark. The dance floor had been crowded. On the other hand, in a sea of more muted colours, Willow's yellow dress drew attention and her eye-catching hair—so thick and soft and silky wrapped around his fingers—shone like a beacon.

But no.

He was being idiotic. He had nothing to worry about. Even if anyone had seen him lose his head, they wouldn't risk his displeasure by gossiping about it. Many there tonight had lucrative business dealings with him. The rest sought them. There was no cause for concern. On that front, at least. Walking out on his sister's wedding, however? That would not have gone unnoticed—at least, not by his family—which was yet another thing he'd no doubt have to deal with in the morning.

Leo sat back against the butter-soft leather and rubbed his eyes, a wave of weariness washing over him. He could sleep for a week. But he was flying to New York tomorrow evening to discuss a potential shipping merger that would add billions to the company's bottom line, so that wasn't happening. Once he'd tied things up there, he had a series of board meetings in London to host. And at some point he'd have to put a stop to the unveiling of a portrait that might well make him a global laughing stock if it went on show. Relaxing, taking some time out, was but a distant dream.

As was peace and seclusion clearly, because barely had Stavros taken his place behind the wheel when the other back door of the car suddenly flung open, shattering the silence and jolting him out of his thoughts. A second later, in a blur of colour, movement and sparkle, into the car and onto the seat slid Willow.

Leo jerked upright, his muscles rigid with tension. His heart crashed against his ribs and a powerful combination of shock and alarm pummelled through him.

What the hell?

'Hi,' she said with one of those dazzling smiles that had too often stunned him into speechlessness, but to which now, thanks to the swift reconstruction of his iron-clad control back there on the dance floor, he was immune.

'Get out.'

'That's rude.'

He stared at her, barely able to believe his ears. She had a nerve. 'What's rude is you ambushing me in my car and invading my space.'

'Needs must.'

He clenched his jaw. 'What do you want, Willow?'

'I was hoping you might be able to give me a lift.'

No. Absolutely not. It was out of the question. The back of his car, which he'd always considered airily spacious, suddenly felt unnervingly claustrophobic. When she'd hopped in, the oxygen had whooshed out. Her scent filled his head. Despite the ample width of the seat, he could feel the hot energy she radiated. And something else. Something that had the hairs on the back of his neck quivering and his pulse racing, which he needed like a hole in the head.

Ignoring the entire bloody lot of it, Leo

reached into his jacket pocket and extracted his phone. 'I'll call you a cab.'

At that, Willow frowned. 'No, no,' she said, shaking her head, which made the beads in her hair catch the overhead light and twinkle. 'That's no good at all.'

'Too bad.'

'Where are you going?'

'To bed.'

'That will do.'

She settled back and made herself comfortable and he had to dig deep to quell both the furious frustration that surged inside him at her intransigence and the volcano of heat that erupted at the thought of her in his bed. 'Are you going to do as I ask and get out of my car?'

'No.'

Having shoved his phone back in his jacket pocket, Leo leaned forwards, pressed a button on the panel that separated the back from the front and said in English, 'Stavros, please take Miss Jacobs wherever she wishes to go. I'll walk.'

He turned to yank open the door, practically tasting fresh air and freedom, when suddenly her body slammed into his back and her hand landed on his arm. Leo froze. His senses reeled.

Willow was curled around him in the darkness, and he could barely breathe.

'OK, wait,' she said, so close her warm breath tickled his neck while his arm appeared to be on fire. 'Forget the lift. It was just an excuse. I wanted to talk to you.'

He didn't need to know. He didn't *want* to know. There'd been too much talking for one night already. What he wanted was to shake her off and get out of the damn car, even if such a dramatic move did attract the attention of the guests trickling out of the hotel to make their own way home. But her proximity and her touch were pulverising his reason and clawing at his control so instead he heard himself saying, 'What about?'

'About carrying on where we left off. On the dance floor. About doing as your brother suggested and getting a room.'

There was a rushing in his head. A pounding in his chest. And all he could think was *Yes, yes, yes* until into the madness, thank God, plunged a much-needed arrow of cold, hard discipline.

Steeling himself, he removed her hand from his arm and abruptly shifted around to make her scuttle back. 'No.'

'Why not?' she said, to his irritation barely

moving at all. 'You seemed pretty into it.' Her gaze dropped to his mouth and her face filled with a dreamy sort of hunger that tightened his chest for a moment. 'That kiss was something else.'

'The kiss was nothing,' he said bluntly, refusing to allow the scorching memory of it into his head and instead offering up heartfelt thanks to whoever had made the decision to tint the car's windows.

'It wasn't. I felt you. Hard. Against me.'

The area in question throbbed and his pulse skipped a beat, but Leo squared his jaw even more and ignored both in favour of a lie. 'It was merely an instinctive response to the environment.' An anathema, in other words. Because, generally speaking, nothing he did was instinctive and he was never affected by an environment. A blip. That was what that moment on the dance floor had been. A momentary lapse after a very stressful day. 'It was nothing out of the ordinary.'

'Don't be so modest.'

The faint smile tugging at her lips fired his mounting irritation at her continued refusal to do as he commanded. 'You're finding this amusing.'

'Not at all,' she said with enviable aplomb.

'I simply know what I want and am intent on getting it.'

'Reverse our roles and this conversation would border on harassment. In fact, it does, even as things stand.'

'Reverse our roles and we'd be naked already because I'd put up no resistance.'

Despite his best efforts, Leo had no defence against the images that cascaded into his head then. They were too many and too vivid. Bodies glued together. Mouths joined, limbs entwined, glorious multicoloured hair spread out on the pillow or swishing down the length of his body. Heat, sweat, breathy moans and soft little cries. In his mind's eye, he could see and hear it all.

'You're playing with fire,' he warned, his voice rough and thick with the desire that, to his consternation, he was struggling and failing to keep at bay.

A glowing light shimmered and danced in the depths of her emerald eyes. 'Is that a threat or a promise?'

Either. Both. He didn't know. 'A threat.'

'I'm OK with getting burned.'

'Are you?'

'Yes,' she said. 'I am very OK with it. In fact, I positively *yearn* to get burned.'

She might think that, but she had no idea that deep inside him lurked the well-buried traces of the youth he'd once been, the fierce, fearless kid who threw tantrums and took risks and crashed boats. No idea what might result if he relinquished his tightly held grip on his control entirely and those traces broke free of the bonds that shackled them to smash to pieces his veneer of civility and take over. Hell, since it had never happened before, even he had no idea of the raging wildness he could be capable of as an adult and the fallout it could incur unleashed. Burning might be the least of it.

'Forget it.'

'One night, Leo,' she said softly, seductively, stealing his wits and scattering his objections to the wind. 'That's all I want. Truly. I can't imagine I'm your usual type. I doubt I'm nearly chic or sophisticated enough for a worldly yet cynical billionaire like you. Relationships aren't my thing and besides, I have my career to focus on. One night together, I'll leave in the morning and you need never see me again. It's nothing to get worked up about. It's just sex. But if you truly have a problem with that, if you really want me to get out of this car and leave you alone, I will.'

She stopped, waiting breathlessly, the pulse

at the base of her neck pounding, and all he could think in the thick thunderingly silent darkness was that he wanted nothing less than to be left alone. He wanted her beyond comprehension, beyond reason, and he couldn't deny it any longer.

There'd been an inevitability to this conversation from the moment she'd invaded his space and shattered his peace. He'd had many opportunities to exit the car and leave her to it yet he'd taken none of them. So what was the point of continuing to fight a battle he'd already lost? And why would he even want to when it had been so long since he'd done something purely for himself?

He'd been overthinking things, that was the trouble. He'd been unsettled by the strength of the desire Willow aroused in him and what that might imply. But it needn't imply anything. He wouldn't lose his head. He never had with a woman before.

And of course he didn't have a problem with a one-night stand, even though for him it would be a first, which was odd, come to think of it, considering he'd got through his fair share of the opposite sex in his younger days. Sure, such behaviour seemed rash and reckless by its very nature and spontaneity hadn't been a word in his vocabulary for years, but he could see the merit in one now. Unaddressed, the relentlessly erotic dreams he'd been having in which she featured so heavily would drive him demented. Addressed, by sunrise, the desire with which he burned could be assuaged and the status quo by which he lived could be restored.

One night spent engaged in the pursuit of ecstasy with a gorgeous, sexy woman who wanted the same...

Maximum pleasure, minimal conversation, no aftermath...

And why, exactly, was he resisting?

'All right,' he growled, all the reasons as to why this was a bad idea wiped out by thoughts of what lay ahead, which accelerated his pulse and hardened his body. 'Fine. Just one night.'

With one last dark, smouldering glance in her direction, Leo hit the button in the panel again and said in Greek something that Willow supposed went along the lines of 'Change of plan—drive us to my house,' and swamped her with relief.

The intended outcome of their conversation had been touch-and-go for a while. Leo had put up quite the opposition, although she had no idea why. She obviously had limited experience, but how many men turned down the offer of no strings attached sex? Not many, she was willing to bet.

But whatever had been going in his head, he'd succumbed in the end. Her instinct, which had told her she hadn't imagined the heat of the kiss and that despite his accusations of harassment he really didn't come across as the sort of man who could be coerced into doing anything he didn't want to do, had been right. Embracing tenacity instead of deliberating for too long and losing one's nerve was definitely the way forward.

Leo was broodingly silent as the sleek car slid smoothly through the dark streets of the city. He stared out of the window, tight of jaw and rigid of body, although whether that was because he was still annoyed at the result of the conversation or simply didn't trust himself to look at her was anyone's guess.

Willow tried to settle into the seat, but she was so aware of him, of every breath he took and every move he made, that it was impossible to relax. Her imagination, even though it had nothing to base anything on, was running riot. If not for the presence of the clearly unflappable Stavros on the other side of the partition she'd have scooted over to Leo's side of the seat and made a start on the night ahead already.

'So where are we going?' she said, partly to cut through the sizzling tension, partly because it was a question she should probably have asked earlier.

'Kolonaki,' he muttered, his gaze fixed on the world of elegant shadowy buildings and bright city lights beyond the window. 'I have an apartment there.'

'Is it far?'

'Ten minutes.'

Willow shivered. A ten-minute build-up and then, pow! She could hardly wait. 'Where's home?' she asked, deciding that time might pass more speedily with conversation than silence, however sticky.

'Santorini.'

'Have you lived there for long?'

'A couple of years. On and off.'

'Selene said the business has offices all over the world.'

'Hundreds of them.'

'As CEO you must travel a lot.'

'I do. Tomorrow evening, I'm flying to New York.'

'Don't worry,' she said, getting the message

loud and clear. 'I'll be long gone by then. What are you doing there?'

'Discussing a merger.'

'From one merger to another.'

He slid her a heavy-lidded glance that fired every nerve ending she possessed. The most devastating smile played at his mouth, a glint appeared in his eye, and suddenly her stomach was flipping about all over the place. 'Quite.'

'So,' she said, scolding herself for responding so absurdly to a mere glint and a smile. 'Is there anything you want to know about me?'

'Are you always this nosy?'

She wasn't, but she didn't much care. Conversation was not only passing the time, it was also keeping her nerves under control, which was a bonus. 'Only with men I'm going to sleep with.'

'And is that a common occurrence?'

It wasn't an occurrence at all. Which was something she should probably admit. Leo had to be far more experienced than she was so he was bound to realise at some point that she hadn't a clue what she was doing. Surely it would be better to clarify the situation and neutralise any issue he may have with it now than in the midst of the action.

'No.' She took a deep breath and mentally

braced herself for what was no doubt going to be a pretty excruciating conversation. 'In fact, this is a first for me.'

There was a beat of silence. The arch of an eyebrow. And then, 'What do you mean?'

'I've never done this before.'

'Issued an indecent proposition? Or had a one-night stand?'

'Both.'

'That makes two of us.'

Interesting, but possibly irrelevant right now. 'I've never actually slept with anyone before either.'

He stared at her in the shadowy darkness, a flicker of astonishment darting across his face. 'You're a virgin?'

'I am,' she confirmed with a nod. 'It's no big deal, obviously. But I thought you should know. In case I do something wrong. I assume you're not.'

'Not since I was sixteen.'

That came as no surprise. He'd probably been as irresistible then as he was now, at the age of thirty-one. How many women had there been in the intervening fifteen years? Why had he never married any of them? Unimportant questions, both of them. All she cared about was the here and now. 'Does my inexperience put you off?'

'No,' he said, but she caught a glimmer of doubt in his eyes, which suggested otherwise and needed to be speedily addressed.

'I hope you're not going to back out because of some antiquated notion of virginity and its value and force me to find someone else.'

'I should.'

'Why?'

'Do you really want your first time to be a one-night stand?'

Yes. That was exactly what she wanted and all she could ever have with the mountainous emotional baggage she carried. Even if she didn't have a giant stumbling block when it came to love, it wouldn't be fair to expect someone to commit to her when her life revolved around her menstrual cycle, when for approximately five days in every month she had to take to her bed, when staying positive was a battle she didn't always win, when she might not be able to ever have children.

Should she tell Leo about the physical baggage she also came with? Despite her conviction that sex with him would be fabulous, there was the chance it might not be and he perhaps ought to be alerted to that possibility. On the other hand, disclosing her virginity and persuading him it didn't matter was turning out to be risky enough. What if her endometriosis—on top of everything else—proved to be a tipping point and he simply figured that she was too much hassle?

No. She wouldn't do anything to jeopardise the night ahead, and that level of emotional intimacy wasn't necessary or appropriate for a one-night stand anyway. Of course everything would be fine. And if it wasn't, well, really, how bad could it actually be?

'I don't much care how it happens,' she said, clearing her head of these discombobulating thoughts and focusing instead on eradicating any reservations Leo might have. 'I just want fireworks. Our kiss on the dance floor suggested that you can provide them. Not all women get to say that about their first time.'

'You're basing a lot on a kiss.'

'I've had dozens of kisses. None of them like that. Have you ever had any complaints?'

'Not to my knowledge.'

'I didn't think so. I know you'll give me what I want, Leo. I trust you to show me stars.'

One agonisingly long second ticked by, then another.

'Would you really find someone else?' he eventually asked with an assessing tilt of his head.

Of course she wouldn't. She'd never met anyone who affected her the way he did, who transported her to a level of pleasure where pain couldn't possibly exist. She certainly wasn't willing to take a risk on this with just anyone. But she wasn't having him back out now, and the way he'd seen off his brother earlier suggested he had a competitive, possessive and possibly even jealous streak.

'Absolutely,' she lied, mentally crossing her fingers. 'I'm twenty-four. It's beyond a joke.'

He seemed to consider this for a moment, undoubtedly weighing up the pros and cons, then said in a voice that was low, gruff and sent delicious tingles to places she didn't know she had, 'Everyone deserves fireworks.'

Relieved beyond belief, Willow inwardly grinned. Excitement churned through her. Her heart pounded. This was going to be, without question, the most exciting night of her life. 'They do indeed.'

CHAPTER FIVE

ANY QUALMS LEO might have had about bedding a virgin had vanished the minute Willow mentioned having to find someone else. The thought of it had boiled his blood and once again, the words *hell, no* had flashed through his head. He didn't know why. Possessiveness wasn't his thing. He'd never once warned Zander off anyone, and he didn't get a kick from the thought of being the first man to show Willow what her body was capable of. He wasn't that unreconstructed a male.

Perhaps the strength of his reaction was down to the certainty that he—and only he—could provide the fireworks she wanted. As unlikely a pairing as they were on paper, their chemistry was exceptional and unique. Or maybe it was because the fact that she trusted him made him feel he could take on the world. Either way, it didn't much matter. The deal was sealed.

He couldn't begin to fathom how she was still a virgin when she looked the way she did, oozed such confidence and flirted so adeptly, but it was nothing to be concerned about. In fact, it could turn out to be a blessing. He'd have to proceed with caution and exercise restraint. He wouldn't be able to lose control even if he wanted to, which, as always, he absolutely did not.

While Leo's thoughts turned to the many things he planned to do to Willow once in close proximity to a bed, Stavros swung the car off the road, drove through a pair of gates and down a tunnel that led to the underground car park. The minute the car came to a halt, Leo sprang out of it, heart pounding, body primed, and strode around the back to the other side. He yanked open the door and held out his hand, which Willow immediately took, exiting the car with far more decorum than he had. He muttered a curt *kalinikta* to Stavros and then marched her to the lift. One quick press of his forefinger to the reader and the doors opened with a soft swoosh. He hustled her in and a moment later they closed, shutting out everything but her and him and the night to come.

The air within the confined space seemed to vibrate with taut anticipation, the electricity sizzling between them practically visible. Her scent, even more intense now than in the car, enveloped him and seeped into him, winding around every fibre of his being. She stood so close they were almost touching. He could feel her heat. Sense her urgency. But he wouldn't touch her. Not yet. He could hold on for the ten seconds it would take for the lift to reach his apartment. Of course he could. He wasn't an animal.

At least he wasn't until he made the mistake of casting her a quick sideways glance. One look at the deep flush on her cheeks, the rapid rise and fall of her chest and the scorching haze of desire in the eyes that were gazing into his and all his good intentions evaporated. To know that she wanted him as much as he wanted her pulverised what few wits he'd been clinging on to, and whether he turned to her first or she turned to him, he neither knew nor cared. All that mattered was that one minute they were staring at each other, as if frozen in time, and the next, something snapped and they were plastered against each other, mouths colliding, teeth clashing, hands everywhere.

As the kiss heated and deepened, Leo backed Willow up against the wall of the lift and pinned her in place with his hips. She melted against him and moaned. The wave of lust that rolled over him nearly took out his knees. His heart pounded. His ears popped. His blood rushed round his body like liquid fire.

Becoming dimly aware that the doors had opened—when had that happened?—Leo wrenched his mouth from hers, shifted his hold on her and scooped her up. He didn't allow himself to be derailed by her breathy gasp of surprise that would have had him depositing her on the nearest flat surface, which was the floor. Or by the fact that, having zero time for romance and all the fraught messy emotions that came with it, this was the first time he'd ever held the soft warm weight of a woman in his arms. It didn't occur to him to offer her a drink or something to eat. He simply carried her straight down the wide shadowy hall and into his bedroom at the end of it.

'That was very masterful,' she said breathlessly once he'd reached the bed and reluctantly lowered her to the floor.

'I was going for efficient, but I'll take masterful.'

'What do I do?'

Leo's heart thudded. His mouth dried. He'd never experienced anticipation like it. He was so hard he hurt. So addled with desire he was incapable of issuing instructions. 'Whatever you want.'

Willow tilted her head and bit her lip, as if thinking it through for a moment. Then she put her hands to the buttons of his shirt and started undoing them from the bottom up. Every time her fingers brushed against his skin, his muscles flinched and he hissed out a breath.

'I know I said I wanted to draw you,' she said softly as she pushed his shirt and jacket off his shoulders and down his arms, 'but I think I'd rather sculpt you. You are constructed quite magnificently. You'd look exceptional in marble.'

'Thank you. I think.'

However, with her hands running so lightly and teasingly over his torso it was becoming increasingly impossible to think full stop. Especially when she brushed a thumb over his nipple and then leaned forwards to lick it.

'Are you sure you haven't done this before?' he said, his voice thick and hoarse.

'I'm just doing what I want,' she murmured against his skin. 'It was your idea.'

And a mistake, in hindsight. Because he could feel her touch everywhere, like a brand, and it was undoing him so fast he was a hair's breadth from picking her up again and tossing her onto the bed.

Gritting his teeth and ruthlessly resisting the urge to do exactly that, he batted her hand away and pulled her into his arms instead. He buried one hand in her hair and caressed her satiny smooth bare back with the other and kissed her until she was letting out the soft little moans he'd so easily imagined and pressing against him even more tightly.

In response to the rocketing need to be skin to skin, Leo slipped his hands beneath the drapey straps of her dress. As he drew them down her arms, the bodice slithered to her waist and then, with a minute wiggle of her hips, to the floor.

'This dress just gets better and better,' he muttered as she stepped out of it and then stood there in nothing more than gold heels and white lace knickers.

'There's less of it than I'd have liked.'

'Why waste fabric?' He felt a tremble ripple through her, stilled for a second, and frowned. 'Are you all right?'

'I'm fighting the urge to cover myself up like the virgin I am.'

'Nervous?'

She swallowed hard and gave a tiny nod. 'A little.'

His heart thumped. 'Are you having second thoughts?'

'Not a chance.'

'You can back out at any time.'

'I won't.'

'*Theos*, you're beautiful.'

'So are you.'

'Get on the bed. Keep the heels.'

Doing as he instructed, for once, Willow sank onto the bed and shifted up it, the moonlight spilling into the room turning her hair to silver and her skin to pearl. Leo kicked off his shoes and stripped off his trousers, shorts and socks with far more haste than elegance, dizzyingly aware she was watching his every move. Her gaze lingered on his erection and she let out a little raspy sort of sigh, which, ridiculously yet inevitably, made it swell and harden even more.

He came down beside her and rolled over her. His mouth fused to hers, her eyes fluttered shut and with a moan, she lifted her arms to his neck. She ran her hands across his shoulders and over his back and his muscles twitched at the contact. She hitched her knee up and shifted to fit herself better against him.

With desire drumming hot and hard inside him, Leo planted his hand on her leg and ran it up her silky-smooth thigh. He skimmed over the dip of her waist to her breast, and she arched into him. Desperate to taste more of her, he wrenched his mouth from hers and trailed it down her neck and over the gentle slope of her chest. When he closed it over her tight, hard nipple, she gasped and dug her fingers into his hair.

He could feel her trembling. Her ragged little pants stoked his need to unbearable levels. But he couldn't lift himself up and thrust into her as he so badly wanted to. He had to take his time, even if it killed him.

Focusing solely on her and her reactions, Leo slid his hand down her taut abdomen and slipped it beneath the waistband of her pants. Instinctively or not, the knee she'd hitched up fell back, granting him better access to her slick heat, issuing an invitation he could not possibly refuse. He pressed his fingers against the centre of her pleasure and she jerked for a moment before relaxing and breathing, 'Oh, my God.'

She pulled his head up and crushed her mouth to his, kissing him deeply and passionately while her hips began to respond to the movements of his fingers. His head spun as he slipped them inside her. His pulse hammered.

She gasped and groaned and within moments she was panting and throwing her head back and crying out his name as she came apart in his arms, faster and harder than he could possibly have envisaged.

'OK?' he said, thinking he'd never seen anything so magnificent as he watched her recover and wondering if he'd ever forget the sight of it.

She gave him a languid smile that tightened his chest in the oddest way. 'I've never felt so good in my life.'

'It gets better.'

'I don't see how it could.'

'Just wait.'

He moved away from her to locate and apply a condom, which took an age since his hands were shaking so badly and required more self-control than he'd ever imagined he possessed. Then he returned to her, his pulse racing at the excitement that glowed in her eyes and the flush on her cheeks. He parted her legs and positioned himself at her entrance and as he captured her mouth in a searing kiss, pushed into her as slowly and carefully as he could, noting her response, hearing her sharp, shuddery gasp, allowing her time to adjust.

Once lodged inside her, he held himself still so she could get used to the unfamiliar feel of him, every muscle he possessed rigid with the effort of restraint. She was so tight, so hot, so wet. He'd never experienced anything like it. His heart pounded. Need roared through him. His control was hanging on by a thread that was fraying by the second, but he clung on to it, because he would not give in, he would not allow his baser instincts to dominate, until she shifted and took him in further and suddenly something inside him snapped.

An overwhelming need to move gripped every cell in his body. He craved the delicious friction of his flesh sliding against hers with a desperation he couldn't contain. His vision blurred and his head spun. He had to be in her deeper and harder, and as he helplessly succumbed to the drugging desire, she felt so incredible, so unbelievably good, he was losing what was left of his mind.

But then, suddenly, she was twisting her head to the side, pushing at his shoulders, his chest, struggling to dislodge him and kick him off. She was sobbing, 'Stop. Please. Stop,' and everything in him and around him, his body, his heart, the room, *everything,* instantly froze.

In response to the plea that tore from her mouth, Leo jerked as if struck, immediately pulled out of her and reared back. Despite the moonlit shadows, Willow could see that he was as white as the sheets tangled around them. Horror and confusion replaced the wild heat and fierce concentration that had dominated his expression a moment ago, and as she instinctively winced at the acute discomfort of his sharp withdrawal, she wished with all her heart that she hadn't had to call such an abrupt halt to the proceedings.

She'd been having such a good time. The flattering urgency with which he'd yanked her from the car and bundled her into the lift had heated the desire simmering inside her to boiling point. When he'd swept her into his arms and carried her through his apartment to his bedroom, she could have swooned. She'd had a sense of space and air, of high ceilings, thick curtains and ornate decoration, but then he'd removed her dress and his clothes and that had been that for coherent thought. Her nerves had simply melted away. There'd been nothing remotely ice-cold or robotic about him then. She'd never felt so desired.

She'd been right about trusting him to give her what she'd so desperately wanted. The fierce need that had blazed in his eyes as he'd joined her on the bed had set her on fire. The orgasm he'd wrung from her—so much better anything she'd managed herself—had been mind-blowing, and the intense pleasure she'd experienced had gone on and on.

But she'd been wrong about it being enough because when he'd thrust into her, God, it had hurt. She'd felt as if she'd been impaled on a red-hot poker. She'd willed the stabs of needle-sharp pain to lessen, to disappear altogether, hoping against hope that they related to her inexperience, but then he'd started moving and they hadn't. To her distress, they'd worsened, the searing pain spreading a throbbing ache to her abdomen, demolishing the desire and dominating her thoughts, and she simply hadn't been able to bear it.

How naive she'd been to assume that everything would be fine, despite all she knew about her condition. How she wished she'd told him about it back in the car when she'd had the opportunity. She'd been right to be scared all along. Right to avoid sex. She should never have tried to convince herself otherwise. But regret and analysis would have to wait. She had a man in a state of shock to deal with.

'I hurt you,' Leo said gruffly, staring down at her, stunned, clearly appalled, before lifting himself completely off her and jerkily moving away.

Grabbing a sheet and pulling it over herself, Willow rolled onto her side and instinctively curled into the foetal position in an attempt to ease the pain.

'Well, yes,' she admitted, as to her relief the stabbing began to fade. 'But it wasn't—'

'I'm sorry.' He swung round to sit on the edge of the bed, his broad back to her, and shoved hands that looked to be shaking through his hair.

'It's not your fault.'

'I was too rough.'

What? 'No,' she said firmly. 'That's not it at all. Really.'

'I can't believe I missed something,' he said hoarsely.

'You didn't miss anything. Honestly.'

'I should have been more considerate. More patient.'

'You were everything I'd hoped for.'

Even she could hear the sincerity and urgency in her voice, but he obviously wasn't listening to her. It was as if he'd retreated into his own world, a world of misconception and, perhaps, guilt, which she suddenly felt the pressing need to address, whether he heard her or not, because she was not having him thinking he was to blame for this. This was *her* fault.

The pain that had crucified her earlier had dulled to a bearable ache and she uncurled herself, sat up and took a deep breath. 'What just happened is nothing to do with you, Leo,' she said, actually rather glad he had his back to her for the very personal and potentially mortifying explanation she was going to have to give. 'It really isn't. It's me. I have endometriosis. It's a condition where tissue similar to the lining of the womb grows in other places, like the ovaries and things. A nightmare. Anyway. One of the many hideous side effects can be painful sex. That's one of the reasons why I'm—or at least, *was*—a virgin. I already experience quite a bit of pain every month and the risk of more never appealed. But then you kissed me on that dance floor and suddenly none of that seemed relevant. I've never met anyone who turns me on the way you do. You just have to look at me to make me melt. You short-circuit my brain with the slightest of touches. I really had hoped that with you it would be OK. I really wanted it to be and maybe if I'd had more experience it would have been. I'm devastated beyond belief it wasn't.'

She stopped to give him the chance to respond. To perhaps accept her apology and thank her for her explanation. He might request more information and assure her he understood. More likely, he'd renew his offer to call her a cab and send her on her way, which would also be acceptable, if disappointing. But he didn't do anything. He just sat there in the silvery moonlit silence that tautened and thickened with every passing second, and it was every bit as awful as she'd feared.

What was he thinking? That she was a freak? A tease? An object of pity? She didn't want to know. In fact, right now, all she wanted was to go. She was feeling cold and embarrassed and horribly vulnerable. The loss of her virginity and the stunning orgasm she'd had now counted for nothing. Fire had turned to ash. Leo was still utterly frozen, apparently oblivious to her, his head in his hands, and it was excruciating.

'I realise this isn't what you signed up for,' she said, swallowing down the lump in her throat with difficulty. 'This wasn't the deal we made. If anyone should apologise, it's me. I didn't think it would be an issue, but I should have at least warned you it could be. I'm really sorry I didn't. I'm really sorry this happened.'

Gutted, disappointed and humiliated at the

way the night had ended, but also deeply relieved she'd never have to see him and face this again, Willow eased off the bed and slipped on her dress.

'Have a good trip,' she said, and without looking back, she fled.

Generally speaking, Leo had little time for regret. He wasn't rash. Every decision he made was deliberately and lengthily considered, so he knew beyond doubt that it was the right one to take at the time. Therefore, he rarely looked back to contemplate whether he could or should have done something differently, even on the extremely rare occasion he made the wrong call.

However, over the course of the next few days, whether discussing the merger in New York, sitting through the series of interminable board meetings in London or ignoring Zander's puerile texts about the dance floor kiss and his siblings' interest in his premature exit from the wedding, he came to deeply regret the way the night with Willow had ended.

He had not handled it well. That he'd been so stunned and horrified at the thought he'd hurt her he hadn't been able to even think straight, let alone respond to what she'd told him—most of which had been muffled by the white noise in his head anyway—was no excuse. He should have found a way through the chaos. He should have asked her to repeat what she'd told him and explain it in more detail.

How he could have allowed her to leave like that, to emerge onto the dark city streets and make her way back to wherever she was staying, alone and in pain, he had no idea. That wasn't him. He took care of those around him. He did everything in his power to prevent anguish. Or so he'd always believed.

Whenever he thought of the events of that night—which was pretty much 24-7—he broke out into a cold sweat. He couldn't get the memory of Willow begging him to stop out of his head. The desperation in her voice cut through his thoughts like a knife. How had he not noticed her discomfort? How long had she put up with it before becoming unable to take any more and pushing him off? What madness had driven him to such, well, *madness*? Chemistry? Genetics? What?

From time to time over the years, Leo had wondered what the fallout might be if he ever lost control. He'd assumed that once the spinning plates had smashed on the ground he'd be exposed for the fraud he suspected he was.

He'd imagined that as before, the emotions he kept such a tight lid on would burst free and the resentment he still bore deep down would surge up. Mistakes with regard to the business would once again be made and the family's fortunes would flounder. But he'd never imagined that he could be capable of causing someone pain—all his adult life he'd striven to do the opposite—and the resultant guilt at having done so was unbearable.

So if he had any sense at all, he'd track Willow down and apologise properly for both what he'd done and how he'd dealt with it. He'd throw himself on her mercy and beg her for forgiveness, and then he might finally get some peace.

But he didn't.

Because, despite all that, drawing a line under everything and consigning her to history didn't feel right. He still dreamed of her. He still wanted her. The fact that she'd chosen him over anyone else to relieve her of her virginity burned a trail through his brain, along with the revelation that he melted her with a look and frazzled her thoughts with a touch.

He didn't like the notion that a passionate vibrant woman like her was unable to experience the heady delights of great sex. He didn't appreciate the feeling of failure or the fact that the impression she had of him now had to be less than favourable. Their business felt unfinished, the mistakes he'd made clawed at his gut, and all he could think about was reparation.

So he wouldn't be banning the unveiling event that he'd learned from Atticus his mother was planning. In fact, he'd be attending it. It would provide the perfect opportunity to talk to Willow, which he might not get otherwise. And quite frankly, a couple of hours of discomfort at having to come face-to-face with the work that had given him sleepless nights was a small price to pay for the chance to right so many wrongs.

CHAPTER SIX

FOR THE UNVEILING of her portrait—which, to Willow's surprise and relief, had gone ahead without any intervention—Selene had commandeered the top floor of an exclusive Athens nightclub and rustled up two hundred of her closest friends. Willow had no clue how she'd achieved either with such short notice but presumably those were the perks of being rich and infamous.

Eight days had passed since the disastrous night she'd spent with Leo. It had taken her some time and a concerted effort to be able to think of it without squirming with embarrassment and overheating, but keeping busy had helped. There'd been this evening to prepare for and the contacts she'd made at the party to follow up on.

Going home to her studio in London when there was so much to do here and so little time in which to do it hadn't made sense, but the downsides of staying in Athens in the interim, of course, were the constant reminders of the society wedding of the year. The newsstands were filled with magazines that bore official photos of the bride and groom on the cover. It was only through sheer willpower that Willow had managed to resist the temptation to buy one. She had no desire to see if Leo featured within. She had business and a career to attend to and a night of regret and humiliation to cast into oblivion for good.

Fortunately for that goal, there was no danger of him showing up here tonight and bringing it all back up again. The portrait was huge, spotlit and centre stage. She'd been interviewed and photographed for half a dozen international publications already and one person after another had come up to compliment her on her work. But while she was practically bursting with pride and delight at the response, tonight's unveiling had to be Leo's worst nightmare made real. Which was a shame, really, because no one was gossiping, no one was sniggering, and if only he could get over his issues with it, he'd see that the portrait truly was a—

'So this is it.'

At the sound of the deep, gravelly voice a

foot to her right, Willow nearly jumped out of her skin. She whipped round, her heart pounding as if she'd run a hundred metres in ten seconds, to find the man who'd made no bones about his distaste for the portrait, the man she'd assumed would be a million miles away on a night like this, standing beside her and staring straight at it.

One glance at his strong, stern profile and tall muscled body clad in blue jeans and a loose white linen shirt and the memory of the two of them wrapped around each other on his sheets, him blowing her mind before everything went horribly wrong, flew into her head, blurring her vision and crushing the breath from her lungs.

But she forced it out and blinked and breathed and willed her heartbeat to slow. This was a professional event for her. She had to focus on that. She would not dwell on what had happened in his bedroom or allow a return of the mortification she'd worked so hard to eradicate. She didn't need to know what he'd been doing lately or if he'd thought about her at all and in what context. She was all about looking forwards, and not just at the portrait.

'This is it,' she said coolly.

He examined the work from top to bottom

and then back up again, his expression inscrutable. 'I didn't know my mother owned a throne.'

'It's not just any old throne,' she said, more than happy to keep the conversation solely on the art. 'It's a replica of Louis the Fourteenth's.'

'Of course it is.'

'She had it made specially. To go with the tiara.'

'The tiara originally belonged to my grandmother.'

'So I understand.'

'She was one hundred and fifty centimetres tall and the same wide,' he said with an assessing tilt of his head. 'I can't imagine her in quite such a pose.'

'Selene drapes—and smoulders—very well.'

'She should. She's had plenty of practice.' He leaned forwards and frowned at the tiny red heart on the inner thigh of his mother's right leg, which was hooked over one gilded arm of the ornate throne. 'Is that a tattoo?'

'It is,' she confirmed. 'She had it done two years ago. A birthday present for a former lover. She thought a portrait might be less painful this time.'

The one eyebrow she could see rose. 'Less painful for whom?'

Willow bit her lip to prevent the smile that

developed at Leo's wry observation since he still hadn't said what he thought of the piece and for some reason that was annoying.

'Lazlo likes it,' she said, reminding herself yet again that his opinion was as irrelevant as his approval. Her clients—past, present and future—were the only people who mattered. 'He's going to hang it in his bedroom.'

Leo grimaced. 'I know,' he said. 'I saw him when I arrived a few minutes ago.'

'You missed his speech. It was very impassioned.'

'I dare say I can live with the disappointment.'

'Given your antipathy towards the work, I am rather surprised you didn't try and put a stop to this evening.'

'That was the original plan.'

'What happened?'

'The plan changed.'

'With your need for order and control, that must have been irritating.'

The glimmer of a smile hovered at his sensual mouth. 'You'd think so, wouldn't you?'

'So is it as bad as you feared?' she asked, giving up all pretence of indifference because she might as well admit she badly needed to know one way or another. 'The picture, I mean.'

'Not quite,' he replied after a moment's consideration. 'Obviously, it's not something I'd have on my wall, but you were right. It *is* tasteful. And unexpectedly beautiful. You are exceptionally talented.'

The intense delight that spun through her at his praise nearly took out her knees. She filled with the disturbing urge to throw herself at him and smother him in kisses, which was bizarre. She remained where she was and offered up a small smile instead. 'Thank you.'

'What made you choose portraits?'

'Because I'm better at them than anything else. I feel a stronger connection with animate objects.'

'And why pastels?'

'I like the luscious velvety texture they achieve. The colours are deep and rich and easy to blend. The luminosity they can create is magical. And on a practical level they're easy to cart around, which was useful when I had to bring them to Athens. It'll make the new commissions I've taken on logistically more manageable, too. Shockingly,' she added dryly, 'your friends and acquaintances don't want to come to a tiny studio in London. They expect me to travel to them.'

'That *is* shocking.'

'I know.'

'Have you acquired many new clients?'

'Can you believe I'm booked up for the next twelve months?'

'That doesn't surprise me in the least.'

'Really?'

'Like I said, you're very talented. Although once seen, this particular work of yours can't be unseen,' he mused, shoving his hands in the pockets of his jeans and rocking back on his heels, 'which is something I'll have to get used to.'

'Then why come?'

'I volunteered to take one for the team.'

'The team?'

'My siblings. Daphne's still on honeymoon and strangely enough, the others discovered they had other engagements tonight.'

'That's noble.'

'My motives aren't that altruistic.'

She found that hard to believe. She didn't know him well, but what little she did know suggested he had considered the welfare of those closest to him of paramount importance. 'No?'

'I figured gatecrashing this evening would be a surefire way of seeing you. After how I reacted the night of the wedding, I didn't think you'd grant me an audience otherwise.'

Willow took no notice of the faint twinge of discomfort she felt at his referral to the night she'd worked hard to erase from her memory. Instead, she focused on the fact that he was probably right, although his reasoning was wrong. Her mortification, not his reaction, would have been behind her ignoring any calls he might have hypothetically made.

'Why did you want to see me?' she asked, puzzled by that because as far as she was concerned they were done. 'Why did you want an audience?'

'I have a proposition to put to you.'

He turned to look at her and the impact of his darkly brooding good looks stole the breath from her lungs and the wits from her head. She had to blink to snap the sizzling connection and refocus. 'What sort of a proposition?'

'The sort that changed the plan and would be best discussed somewhere more private,' he said, the sudden gleam in his eye sending a shiver racing down her spine. 'Follow me.'

Faintly unnerved by the gleam and the possible nature of this 'proposition', Willow nevertheless did as Leo instructed since apparently she found his innate authority absurdly attractive and impossible to resist.

Somewhere more private turned out to be the terrace, which was strung with festoon lights and featured glossy planting and intimate seating. It had a spectacular panoramic view of the Parthenon, behind which the sun was setting. Bathed in warm evening light, the two-and-a-half-thousand-year-old shrine to Athena was all soaring columns, golden stone and lengthening shadows, but it was Leo who held her attention. He was a man on a mission and by the time they'd sat down in a secluded booth in the corner at one end of the terrace, her curiosity was at fever pitch.

'What's this all about, Leo?' she asked, the intensity with which he was looking at her electrifying her nerve endings and drying her mouth.

'It's occurred to me recently that we have unfinished business.'

Willow's pulse skipped a beat and her entire body flushed with heat. So much for hoping he'd put the details of that night from his mind as she'd tried to. 'We don't,' she said firmly, not wanting to revisit their so-called unfinished business for so many reasons. 'We really don't.'

'I disagree,' he countered, the set of his jaw

suggesting he was not to be deterred. 'I owe you an apology. For reacting to the situation badly and letting you walk out.' He paused, frowned, then added, 'Most of all, for hurting you in the first place.'

'That's not your fault,' she assured him with an airy wave of her hand, as if she wasn't curling up with embarrassment inside. 'It's all mine. Like I said at the time, I should have warned you it was a possibility.'

'You weren't to know.'

'I was actually. There's little about my condition I *don't* know. I got carried away, which was stupid and naive, in hindsight. You certainly weren't to know, though. I can't imagine you'd ever hurt someone deliberately.'

'I endeavour not to.'

'But if it's that important to you,' she added, needing this cosy little chat to be over for the sake of her composure, 'I accept your apology.'

'Thank you.'

'Excellent. So. Shall we get back to the party?'

She half got up, more than ready to march back into the throng, only to freeze when his arm shot out and his hand caught her wrist for a moment before instantly letting it go as if he'd been burned. 'I'm not finished.'

Drat.

She resisted the urge to shake the tingles from her arm and reluctantly sat back down. 'Oh?'

'I read up on endometriosis.'

Willow hadn't thought it possible to blush any more, but she'd been wrong. Accusations of frigidity and prick teasing would be infinitely preferable to a conversation about gynaecology with a man who epitomised masculinity. 'Why would you do that?'

He arched one dark eyebrow. 'Why wouldn't I?'

'Because firstly, you didn't need to, and secondly, it's girls' stuff.'

'I have three sisters,' he pointed out dryly. 'I am not remotely fazed by "girls' stuff", as you put it. And I did need to. I dislike ignorance. Knowledge is power. Which brings me on to my next point.'

'And that is?'

'According to my research, which was extensive, sex with endometriosis doesn't have to be painful.'

'Not always, no,' she hedged cautiously, wondering where he was going with this, barely able to believe they were discussing it in the first place when she'd only ever talked about it with medical professionals.

'Position and angle can make a difference.'

Her cheeks burned. 'Apparently.'

'Timing, too.'

'For some.'

He leaned forwards, his burnt umber gaze holding hers so compellingly she couldn't look away even if she wanted to. 'So I suggest we try again.'

At that, Willow's heart gave a great thud against her ribs. Was he nuts? Had he forgotten how awkward it had been? 'Why on earth would you suggest that?'

'Because it doesn't seem fair that you're missing out,' he said. 'Because I'm good at solving problems. Because I've never wanted anyone the way I want you. Because I caused you pain, albeit unintentionally, which is causing *me* guilt and I want to make that right. Take your pick.'

Willow ignored the wave of longing that surged through her in response to the realisation that he still wanted her as much as she still wanted him because it was utterly irrelevant now. 'Well, I pick none of the above,' she said firmly. 'Because I'm never having sex again.'

'Right.'

'I'm serious.'

As the realisation that she meant it dawned, Leo's faint smile faded and a deep frown creased his brow. 'You deliberately choose celibacy?'

She nodded. 'Absolutely,' she said, blotting out the clamouring voice of denial in her head since there was no point wallowing in regret and disappointment. At least alone, she'd be safe, free of emotional intimacy and in absolutely no danger of falling in love and ruining lives. 'It's worked for me so far. It will do so again. Millions of people around the world make that choice. It's a perfectly acceptable one.'

'I agree,' he said with a slow nod. 'But not everything about that night was a disaster.'

The memory of what he'd done to her, of how hard and fast she'd shattered in his arms slammed into her head, and her skin tightened. 'No.'

'Don't you want to know what more there could be?'

'Not if "more" is going to hurt like it did.'

'And that's why I think we should experiment,' he said, clearly not to be deterred. 'See what works for you and what doesn't.'

'Why are you doing this?' she said, baffled by his persistence. 'You could have anyone.'

'I don't want anyone. I want you.'

Her heart soared for a moment before reason intervened and planted her back on earth. 'As a problem to solve,' she said. 'Something broken to fix. A project.'

'I still dream of you,' he said, not denying her accusation, she noticed, although with the way his voice had somehow become a caress, seductive and hypnotic, that didn't seem to matter. 'I still find you irresistible. I want your hands on me. Your mouth on mine. Agree to my proposal and as soon as you're finished here, I'll take you to my estate on Santorini. For the weekend. It's very private. It has its own beach. There'll be no distractions there. Nothing to disturb us. We can take it slowly. Carefully. You will be in control.' His gaze dipped to her mouth and his voice dropped an octave. 'Totally in control.'

Him? Give up control? Really? Hmm. 'I find that hard to believe.'

'I'm willing to make an exception for this.'

'Why?'

'Because our chemistry is unique and I want to know what it will be like between us as much as I think you do. We can experiment until we get it right. And imagine getting it right, Willow. Imagine the fireworks.'

Willow didn't need to imagine them. She was experiencing them now. Tiny explosions were detonating in the pit of her stomach and shooting showers of sparks into every centimetre of her body. His eyes were so dark, so compelling, his voice was so shiveringly spellbinding. She wanted his hands on her and his mouth on hers too, with a desperation that ached.

What if he was right? she couldn't help wondering, her resolve wavering wildly in response to everything he'd said. What if it *was* about position and angle and timing? Maybe it had hurt so badly because of where she'd been in her cycle. Or because he'd been on top of her. Or because, it being her first time, she'd tensed at the unfamiliar intrusion, which was never going to make it good.

Right now, she was roughly in the middle of the month and it would never be her first time again. If he genuinely meant what he said—and she couldn't see why he wouldn't—she could be in charge of the pace and position. She trusted him to stop if she needed him to. He had before.

And while she might never be able to embrace commitment, deep down she didn't want a lifetime of celibacy. She wanted the excitement and pleasure he promised to unlock. She longed to explore her sexuality and discover how *she* could be in control of her body instead of the other way round. Physical intimacy didn't have to mean emotional intimacy and for one weekend, surely, she could be brave?

'All right,' she said, her heart thumping with anticipation and hope, the desire she'd kept at bay rushing through her like a river smashing through a dam wall. 'Why wait? Let's go now.'

Making their escape took longer than Leo had anticipated since frustratingly, people kept coming up to talk to him. But within the hour, having picked up a bag from Willow's hotel, he was pulling into the VIP car park that served the private business aviation terminal at Athens Airport, still congratulating himself on a good plan well executed.

Once he'd devoured all the information on her condition he could find, he'd mentally revisited every encounter and conversation he and Willow had shared and begun to strategise. It hadn't been particularly complicated. He'd known what he wanted, and like her, he'd intended to get it, hence setting aside his issues with the portrait and attending its unveiling.

He hadn't doubted the outcome of the conversation on the terrace for a second. He could be extremely persuasive when he chose and most people came to see things his way eventually. That was why he'd had the jet on standby and the villa restocked. His focus had been wholly on the goal, his decisiveness and self-confidence making a welcome return, and after weeks of feeling utterly at sea when it came to this woman, retaking the helm and steering the ship in the direction *he* wanted had felt good.

What *had* taken him by surprise, however, was the degree of satisfaction and relief he'd experienced when she'd acquiesced. It had nearly floored him. Was the guilt he felt over what had happened the night of the wedding reception really that skewering? Did he want her in his bed that badly? Perhaps her presumably negative image of him bothered him more than he'd assumed. Perhaps altruism *was* his thing, after all.

Ultimately, it didn't matter. The weekend was to be purely physical. An opportunity to right so many wrongs and finally draw a line under the month-long blip in his otherwise rock-steady life. Come Sunday evening, armed with proof that great sex *was* possible for her, Willow would head off to conquer the art world and he'd continue to run the family empire to the best of his abilities and protect his siblings from the capriciousness of his mother. The status quo would be restored and his head would never be turned again.

If Willow had been harbouring any doubts about having made the right decision back there on the terrace—which she wasn't, even though her completely irrational response to the tall, polished brunette who'd accosted them on their way out of the nightclub had made her question whether she was absolutely sure she knew what she was doing—they'd have been swept away by the excitement of travelling by private jet. It certainly beat the no-frills experience she'd had on her journey from London to Athens all those weeks ago. Leo's plane came with a dozen large cream leather seats, a crew of six and a magnum of champagne, a glass of which she accepted from a flight attendant with a smile and an appallingly pronounced *efharistó*.

'So this is very comfortable,' she said, taking a sip of deliciously cool bubbles to control the jumble of nerves and anticipation twisting her stomach into knots, and settling back to enjoy the luxury once they were in the air.

Across the polished walnut table, Leo unfastened his seat belt and shot her the glimmer of a smile. 'It's the only way to travel.'

If you were a billionaire, perhaps. For lesser mortals, a pair of feet or a bicycle did just fine. 'Don't tell that to your shipping shareholders.'

'The shipping we do is commercial,' he said, draining his cup of the coffee he'd opted for since he'd be driving from Santorini Airport to the house. 'The transglobal cargo-in-containers sort.'

'No cruise liners? No corporate yachts?'

'Sadly not.'

'That does seem remiss.'

'Don't feel too sorry for me,' he said wryly. 'The planes more than make up for it.'

Planes, plural? 'How many do you have?'

'The family has this one. The company has another three.'

'Handy for getting around.'

And for whisking women off for a weekend of sex at his secluded island villa, such as the beautiful brunette he'd chatted to at the party? They'd seemed pretty friendly. Not that it was any of her business. She wasn't remotely interested in Leo's romantic past. Just as well she wasn't the jealous type, though. Otherwise the urge she'd had to shove the other woman out of the way would have been down to the desire to scratch her eyes out instead of simple annoyance at the delay.

'So who was the brunette?'

Hmm. Perhaps she was more interested than she cared to admit.

A flicker of bemusement flitted across his face. 'What brunette?'

Willow set her glass down on the table and feigned nonchalance. 'Leggy. Gorgeous. Silky white trouser suit. Very pleased to see you as we made our way out of the nightclub. You gave her a kiss on each cheek, rattled away in Greek for a few moments and then she drifted off with a cool smile.' Not that she'd noticed or anything.

'Ah,' he said with a faint nod. 'That was Sophia.'

'A girlfriend?'

'We dated for a couple of months a year or so ago. I haven't seen her since.'

For some reason, that came as a relief. 'She has excellent hair,' Willow said magnanimously. 'Personally, I've never been able to master the art of the chignon.'

Leo ran his gaze over her head and her face, so leisurely and thoroughly that by the time his eyes met hers, her heart was pounding and her mouth had dried. 'Your hair suits you.'

'I'm not sure whether to take that as a compliment or an insult,' she said, taking another sip of champagne to alleviate her parched throat and willing her raging pulse to slow.

'It's a compliment. It's very unusual.'

'Unusual good or unusual bad?'

'Merely an observation,' he said smoothly, the canny brother of three sisters.

Overly warm, her skin prickling, Willow shifted on her seat to alleviate the sensation, a move which nearly resulted in a wardrobe malfunction. 'Have you had many girlfriends?' she asked, adjusting the asymmetric bodice of her one-shoulder navy dress.

'Many before my father died,' he replied vaguely his gaze lingering on her cleavage before returning to hers, a fraction darker and hotter than it had been a moment ago. 'Only some since then.'

'You never appear in the press with any of them.'

'I take great care not to. My private life is private.'

'Why aren't you married?' she asked, the interest she wasn't supposed to be showing apparently overriding his right to privacy.

'I've yet to meet the right woman.'

That came as no surprise. He'd be a hard

man to please. The woman to match his exacting standards probably didn't even exist. 'I got the impression when we first met that you don't have much regard for romantic love.'

'It's not an emotion I'm familiar with.'

'Do you want children?'

'I wouldn't be averse to having a family at some point in the future.'

Which ruled her out. Not that she'd ever ruled herself in, of course. But still, it was good to know where she stood. No point in getting hopes up where regrettably there could never be any.

'And what about you?' he said a little abruptly, breaking into her thoughts before they could drift off into the sorrow and regret she felt whenever she contemplated how different her life could have been if her mother hadn't died. 'What's your issue with relationships?'

Willow pulled herself together and determinedly staunched the flow of dreams of an alternative universe in which she successfully had the operations and, after a string of boyfriends, settled down with a husband to make a dozen adorable babies. 'Who says I have an issue with relationships?'

'You did. In my car. The night of my sister's wedding.'

Ah. He was correct. She had. But she didn't need to give an answer with any great detail. He must have read about the potential fertility issues, the possibility of depression and the general disruption to life associated with endometriosis anyway, and disclosing her complicated feelings towards love and death, which she knew made her sound completely irrational, would necessitate a conversation about her parents' relationship and hers with them that was far too emotionally revealing to have with a man she'd never see again once the weekend was over.

'No time,' she replied with an evasive shrug. 'No opportunity. With everything I've got going on health-wise I am not the world's greatest catch. Although this weekend might change that. Does this plane of yours have a bed?'

'Yes.'

'We could make use of it.'

His dark eyes gleamed. 'We land in fifteen minutes.'

'And?'

'We're going to need hours.'

A bolt of heat speared through her at that and

a wave of desire washed over her but somehow she made herself ignore it all. 'Then you'd better tell me about your brothers and sisters instead.'

CHAPTER SEVEN

IN RESPONSE TO her suggestion, Leo gave Willow a brief potted history of each of his five siblings—focusing on their roles in the business, rather than much in the way of the personal—which did not make for sparkling conversation but did at least keep his mind off the bed in the cabin at the rear of the plane. It was also a vastly preferable topic of conversation than his previous relationships.

He couldn't work out why he'd allowed so many questions to be asked before he'd finally had the presence of mind to shut her down. Insights into their respective feelings about romance—or lack thereof, in his case—had no place in what they were doing here. He'd never shared such personal information with any of the women he slept with, either before or after his father's untimely demise. Yet Willow had moved and her right breast had very nearly come free of her dress and he'd become so preoccupied with not leaping to her side of the table, not putting his hands on her to find out if she was braless, as he suspected, that he'd answered her questions without a second thought.

If he were prone to flights of fancy he'd have assumed she'd cast some sort of spell over him or slipped a drug into his coffee, but he wasn't so he didn't. Instead, as they came in to land, he pulled himself together and reminded himself that this weekend was principally about Willow and her exploring her sexuality.

As he'd informed her earlier, she'd be in charge. It was strange how comfortable he was with that, given his bone-deep need for control, but then the exception he was making for her was a very brief, very minor one. Experience suggested that with her, the results would be stunning. The cost to himself, he was confident, would be zero.

There was no way in hell he was going to repeat the mistakes he'd made before. He was better than the sickeningly self-centred, thoughtless beast he'd briefly turned into the night of his sister's wedding. He'd learned his lesson and he'd use this weekend to prove it to himself and get things back on track. He had a plan, his resolve was rock-solid, and this time, nothing, absolutely *nothing*, was going to go wrong.

As Leo turned off the main road and steered the car down the long windy track to the house, Willow thought that if they didn't arrive at their destination soon she might well explode with need. With every moment that ticked by her imagination grew that little bit wilder, the conversation they'd had on the plane about his family an increasingly distant and blurry memory.

As a result, by the time they passed through a pair of giant gates and travelled up a wide, sweeping drive, desire was bubbling up inside her like a pot on the boil. Her pulse was thundering like a steam train and her ears were buzzing from the pressure.

This was it, was the only thought drumming through her head. Her moment for fireworks and glory and vanquishing her fear of sex. The moment she'd never thought she'd be brave enough to seize.

It was only when he brought the car to a smooth stop in front of the large shadowy structure that the nerves unexpectedly kicked in and an insidious voice in her head suddenly started whispering.

But what if it isn't? What if he's wrong? What if you try and try and it still doesn't work? What would that mean for the future? A lifetime alone? Or what if it does *work but it isn't as good as you're anticipating? Has it crossed your mind that chemistry might not be enough, that with your inexperience the sex might be mediocre? And if it is, how humiliating would that be?*

Leo killed the engine and exited the car, leaving Willow to sit there stock still, the questions clattering around her skull obliterating the desire and quickening her pulse. Her lungs were tightening from the crushing pressure she could feel pressing in on her on all sides and she found she was struggling for breath.

Shakily, she got out of the car, leaned back against it and inhaled the warm salty air until her racing heart slowed and she could once again breathe. While Leo popped the boot and extracted their bags, she took a moment to stare up at the vast canopy of stars above, to listen to the soft, soothing rush of the sea, her jangling nerves quieting and her jumbled thoughts clearing.

Only a moment ago all she'd wanted was to head for a bedroom as fast as possible with the man whose confidence and certainty had blasted her objections to smithereens, who'd promised her a weekend of discovery, a weekend to remember.

But now she was wondering if there was any particular need to be quite so hasty. Maybe the frenzied desperation that had characterised their last encounter had been the trouble. Desire had a habit of erupting without warning. Their kisses became blistering within seconds. On the dance floor... In the lift... So perhaps this time, seeing as how they *had* time, they'd be wise to take things slowly, to deal with the heat cautiously as it ebbed and flowed instead of instantly succumbing to it and drowning.

A bag in each hand, Leo strode to the front door and opened it. Willow pushed herself off the car and followed him on in. After dumping the luggage, he shut the door behind them and voice activated the lights, then turned to her and said, 'What would you like to do first?'

She took a deep breath and willed him to understand. 'I think I'd like a tour.'

If he was being brutally honest, a tour of the house was not what Leo had imagined giving Willow on arrival at his estate. But he'd seen her staring up at the infinite sky as she'd leaned against the car, breathing deeply and steadily.

He'd sensed her tension as she'd stood there in the hall, looking a little pale, and if a tour would settle her apparent nerves, then that was what he'd do. The last thing he wanted was to dive right in, guns blazing, as they were wont to do, and the night to go wrong again. She'd be out the door in a flash and nothing would have been resolved.

As he showed her around the spacious interlinked rooms of the ground floor, she oohed and aahed her appreciation of the space, while he fought the memories of how she'd made similar noises the night she'd come apart in his arms before it had imploded.

In the sitting room, in response to her questions about the house, he muttered something about the appeal of the bright white walls, the clean lines and sharp angles of the unfussy modern building and the serenity and seclusion of the location, and resisted the urge to pull her down with him onto the soft deep sofa.

By the time he stood aside at the vast glass sliding doors so she could step out of the house and onto the terrace that stretched out high and wide above the sea, his muscles were rigid with the effort of keeping his distance and his head was pounding.

'I bet the views are stunning by day,' she

murmured, leaning her elbows on the railing, her body all long lines and soft curves.

'They are.'

'You said you don't get to spend as much time here as you'd like.'

'I don't.'

'That seems a shame.'

What was a shame was that they weren't kissing. But he would not rush. He would not push. He'd promised her control over the proceedings and he would not renege on that. 'The demands made of me are many.'

She straightened and pushed herself off the railing, turning to look at him with an unexpectedly smouldering gaze that made his heart crash against his ribs and nearly took out his knees. 'Can you handle some more?'

'Yes.'

'Then show me upstairs.'

It was Leo's patience that had given Willow the confidence to rein in her nerves and go for what she was now back to wanting quite desperately. By apparently reading her mind and stepping away, both literally and metaphorically, he'd given her the space and time she needed to get her head around the events to come. It had reassured her that whatever happened between them, whether a spectacular success or another abject failure, everything would be all right.

Correctly interpreting her words once again, Leo took her by the hand and led her back through the rooms and up the sweeping stone staircase, the urgency she could feel vibrating off him tempered with restraint. Keeping up when her limbs were as weak as water and her lungs were short of breath was a challenge, but within moments he'd tugged her down the landing and through an open door. One muttered word and the nightstand lights flicked on, and then, before the doubts she'd vanquished staged an unwelcome resurgence and got the better of her, she closed the distance between them and planted her hands on his chest.

As she slid them up, feeling his heart pounding hard and fast beneath her right palm, and wound them around his neck, his arms encircled her waist. She lifted her head at the same time as he lowered his, and their mouths met in a slow, sensual exploration, as if they had all the time in the world, as if he wanted to prove his intention to keep his promise of slow and careful and continue to give her space.

Melting against him, Willow battled the urge to deepen and intensify the kiss. Her head swam, the desire surging and the heat inside her rocketing, and when she felt the hard length of him pressing into her, she longed to fall onto the bed in a tangle of limbs and a wild shedding of clothing. But she stayed where she was, locked in an embrace that was the main course, not merely the starter, and which he seemed in no hurry to end.

When they did eventually sink to the bed— limbs weak, breathing ragged—it was in a smooth glide not a frantic tumble, and the kisses continued, scorching yet languid.

'How do you do this to me?' she breathed when he transferred his mouth to her neck and began to lay waste to the sensitive skin beneath her earlobe.

'I should ask you the same thing,' he murmured, his hot breath making her shiver.

'I guess opposites really do attract.'

'So it would seem.'

He rolled onto his back, deftly taking her with him. With one hand, he threaded his fingers through her hair and pulled her head down for another searing kiss. The other, he slid up back of her thigh, ruching her navy dress as it went, until he reached her bottom.

When he pressed her gently but firmly harder against his erection, Willow moaned softly. She was melting from the inside out. She couldn't get close enough. Her head filled with his scent and her body was awash with heat.

She wanted him inside her so badly she ached, but this was where it had gone wrong before. How she'd felt hadn't been enough. He'd been too much. She'd sensed his desperation and the moment his restraint had snapped. Maybe the depth of his penetration and the power of his thrusts had contributed to her discomfort that night. Maybe there was a way to help with that this time.

Lifting her mouth from his and breathing hard, Willow pushed herself up and shifted until she was sitting astride him. With shaking fingers, she started unbuttoning the buttons of his now badly creased shirt. She pushed the fabric away, set her hands on his warm bronzed skin over which lay a smattering of dark hair and felt a stab of giddy satisfaction when he tensed and hissed out a breath.

She lowered her head and put her mouth to his chest and felt a shudder rip through him. Grappling at the buckle of his belt, she kissed her way down his torso and the rigid muscles of his abs, lingering over the rises and dips of the contours.

'No. Willow,' he muttered, clamping a staying hand over hers when her intentions became obvious.

'How badly do you want me?'

'Can't you tell?'

She could. He was rock-hard beneath her hands. She wanted to feel him, explore and taste him and see if she could make him shatter the way he had her.

'Let me take the edge off it,' she said softly, her heart pounding and her mouth watering at the thought of it. 'You said I'd be in charge and I want to do this. I think it will slow us down. I think it will help. Tell me what you like. Tell me if I'm doing it wrong.'

With a rough groan of defeat, Leo lifted his hips and helped Willow remove his jeans and underwear. He shifted up the bed and fell back against the headboard while she settled between his legs and took him in her hand. Her fingers closed around him and his eyes shut as white-hot darts of pleasure speared through him.

There was nothing she could do wrong. Nothing at all. Every tentative stroke of her fingers, every slow pull of her hand blitzed his brain that little bit more. When he felt her breath on him, his head spun. When her mouth closed over him, his heart nearly leapt out of his chest. He made the mistake of opening his eyes and looking down, and had to grab fist-fuls of sheet to stop himself from thrusting his hands in her gorgeous multicoloured hair and guiding her in the way he wanted.

Not that she needed instruction. If he'd been capable of thought, he'd have marvelled at the way she could read his body, despite her lack of experience. He didn't have to tell her what he liked. Somehow, she instinctively knew.

Somewhere in the dusty recesses of his brain he was dimly aware that this should not be happening, that he ought to be focusing on *her* pleasure, but perhaps she was right. Alleviating the intensity of his need so that he could then take care of hers could well be the right call. From his point of view, it was the best call ever.

The wet heat of her mouth and the loose tickling tendrils of her hair maddened him. His breathing was harsh and fast and shallow and was becoming more so with every passing second. The tension coiling inside him was unbearable. He was moments away from losing it and out of habit he tried to pull her head back, but she wasn't having any of it. To his relief, she simply shook him off and carried on, and he couldn't have protested even if he'd wanted to.

When she increased the exquisite pressure and upped the pace, he lost the ability to think.

He was impossibly hot, shuddering uncontrollably, and then, his control history, his hands in her hair, his climax was upon him, ripping through his body with the force of a wrecking ball. With a groan, he threw his head back and exploded, pulsing relentlessly until he had nothing left to give.

'Well, we know *that* works,' said Willow with a throaty lightness that totally belied the thundering of her heart, the hot achy throbbing between her legs and the intense feeling of triumph sweeping through her.

She pushed herself up onto her knees and brushed the hair from her face. The tang of musky saltiness lingered deliciously on her tongue. Her jaw ached but she didn't care. Leo's dazed expression made her feel as if she'd conquered the world.

His eyes were glazed and his voice, once he'd recovered enough to be able to speak, was thick and slurred. 'That was—you are—astonishing.'

'Was there anything I could have done better?'

'I hope not. I doubt I'd survive it.'

'Good to know.'

'You made me lose control.'

'And how do you feel about that?'

'I'm not entirely sure,' he murmured with a faint frown. 'Unsettled? It seems churlish to complain but I'm supposed to be empowering you.'

'You did empower me. I'll prove it.'

She scooted up his body and leaned forwards to kiss him while settling herself on his lap, her knees either side of his hips, his legs stretched out behind her. Her heart thumped at the feel of him against her, still hard—although not as much as earlier—and her nerves fluttered for a second, but she'd read that this position—one in which she could dictate things—was a good one. All he had to do was lie back and think of Greece. And she was hot, wet, as ready and as brave as she'd ever be.

'Condom?' she breathed in his ear.

Eyes dark and glittering, he reached out and rummaged in the drawer of the nightstand. Giving him some space, Willow slipped her knickers off, and then she was there and he was there, and all that remained was to sink down onto him. But she hesitated. She was too tense, and it definitely wasn't going to work if she didn't relax. Yet the more she tried to relax the tenser she became, which would only make things worse, and God, this was *awful*.

As if sensing her doubts and fears, Leo shifted, removing the possibility of penetration, and to her relief the anxiety instantly eased. He kissed her slowly and thoroughly and within moments she was curling into him and practically purring. He ran his hands over her back, found the zip of her dress and tugged it down. She shivered as he pushed the garment up and over her head, then tossed it to the floor.

His smouldering gaze roamed over her. His breathing slowed. He wasn't lying back and he wasn't thinking of Greece. He was looking at her as though he wanted to devour her, which to her delight, suggested that he was as into this as she was despite her no doubt clumsy efforts to pleasure him.

He cupped her full, heavy breasts and rubbed his thumbs over her hard nipples, and she gasped at the strength of her response. Her skin burned when he held her. A thousand volts shot to her core. Instinctively she arched her back, needing his mouth to replace his hands, and when he took up her invitation, she trembled. The faint prickle of his stubble grazing her skin intensified the sensations. She clung on to his shoulders and gripped his hair.

The heat powering through her veins was hotter than before. The desire flooding her body was greater, more insistent than anything she'd ever known. Coherent thought was fast disappearing. She just had to do it, she just had to be strong and fearless and—

Oh.

She stilled.

She'd done it. Somehow her body, her hips, in particular, had moved of their own accord and he was inside her. Not too deep. Not too hard.

And...it was OK.

Thanks to Leo's patience and understanding, his reading of her mind and his willingness to let her do what she needed to do, the sacrifice of his much-vaunted control for her sake and his care and consideration, there was no pain, just a little discomfort that was dissipating by the second.

A hot tight knot lodged in her throat. Emotion swelled within her and her eyes stung and she was now the one feeling shaken and unsettled. But she swallowed down the knot and blinked back the emotion because she was filling with a clamouring urge to move, and she wanted to focus on that. Encouraged, hopeful, she bit her lip and tentatively rolled her hips, and that was wasn't too bad either. It was actually really quite good.

His eyes were on hers, so close she could make out flecks of gold in the warm brown. Her reflection shimmered in his dilated pupils.

She had the strangest feeling that if she looked hard enough she'd be able to peer into his soul.

What would she find there? she wondered, feeling him swelling and hardening inside her, although he held himself still. And what would he find in hers? Her deep-seated fear of love and heartbreak? The secret, terrible shame of sometimes resenting her mother for dying and destroying her hopes of romance? The agonising conflict of knowing that on the one hand surgery would help physically, but on the other being terrified of going under and also not waking up?

None of that was for his consumption. A meeting of souls was not what this was about. This was about helping her to function in the way she wanted, so she closed her eyes and pressed herself close. She kissed him hard and began to rock.

Leo held her loosely, giving her space to call a halt to the proceedings should she need to, but she was going nowhere. This position was working beautifully. The articles had been right about it putting her in control. Like this, she could adjust and adapt.

The rocking was becoming sensational. Her vision was blurring, her head was spinning and her body was turning into a quivering mass of sensation. Leo's breathing was ragged against her skin. His muscles were taut beneath her fingers. His big body was trembling and his hands were moving over her heated skin increasingly wildly.

The tension gripping her was becoming unbearable, but just when she thought she could stand it no more, he found her nub and caressed it in the way she so badly needed, and the tingles that had started in her toes swept up her legs, her body, her arms. She could feel a tsunami of something hot and insistent rushing towards her and suddenly, without warning, a volcano of pleasure erupted inside her. It rushed like molten lava through her body, shaking her limbs and jerking her head back.

And as she fought for breath, half gasping, half laughing, the fireworks still exploding behind her eyes, she'd never felt so ecstatic, so relieved, so clever.

'What are you doing?'

Sitting cross-legged on the sofa that stood beneath one of the four windows of the bedroom two mornings later, Willow glanced up from the artist's pad in her lap to find Leo lying on his side, propped up on one elbow. He was watching her with a sleepy yet smouldering gaze that, remarkably, had the power to triple her heart rate and rekindle the desire even though after every delicious thing they'd done together recently she ought to have had enough.

'Sketching you,' she said, heroically resisting the urge to ditch the drawing and return to the bed in which they'd spent much of the past glorious thirty-six hours because her body badly needed a break. 'The light here is incredible. Do you mind?'

'Are you planning to put the end result on show?'

'No. This is solely for me. Something to remind me of the weekend. Not that I'm likely to forget it anytime soon.'

'Then I don't mind.' Leo punched his pillow into shape and rolled over onto his front. 'Just don't expect me to pose,' he said, his words muffled by the feathers and fabric. 'I'm barely capable of moving.'

'You can stay right where you are.'

Which was sprawled diagonally across the super king-size bed, naked apart from the white sheet that lay bunched over his buttocks and upper thighs, quite the sight for sore eyes.

The morning sun streamed in through the window, giving his bronzed skin and splendid musculature a lovely iridescent glow. There was no inch of him that she hadn't explored. No part of him that she hadn't tasted. Capturing the salty, satiny heat of his skin and the giddying power of his body on paper was an impossible task, but she was giving it her best shot.

'You look very sexy in my shirt,' he murmured, eyes still half-shut.

Willow smudged a line and shivered in awareness as the soft crumpled linen she'd taken a liking to brushed against her body. 'You look very sexy out of it.'

'What time is it?'

'Around ten.'

'I haven't slept so late in years.'

'We've been busy.'

His mouth twitched with the faintest of smiles. 'I haven't been so busy in years either.'

Was the mighty surge of satisfaction and pride his words invoked normal? Willow allowed herself a moment to preen, then got a grip because it didn't mean she was special or anything. It probably just meant that he rarely had a weekend spare to indulge in such things.

'How do you normally spend your Sunday mornings?' she asked, tilting her head and determinedly studying his right foot, which was as absurdly alluring as the rest of him.

'Generally, I'm in Athens preparing for meetings I then fly to.'

'Such as the merger in New York?'

'Yes. Although *that* morning I spent pacing around the apartment in a state of guilty remorse.'

'You've more than made up for it,' she said, vaguely wondering why she found feet so difficult to capture. 'I had no idea experimenting would be so rewarding.'

'How do you feel?'

Now, there was a question.

Giving up on his big toe, Willow tapped her pencil against her chin and tried to formulate an answer. The last thirty-six hours had been incredible. Once her fears had been overcome and her passion unleashed, she'd been insatiable. So many positions. So much pleasure. Not everything they'd tried had worked for her, but on those occasions, it hadn't been awkward at all. Leo had been endlessly patient and her confidence had rocketed, and she'd begun to ponder the pros and cons of carefully timed, short-lived flings in the future.

'Amazing,' she said, wondering how on earth she could sum up the myriad emotions rushing around her system. 'Relieved. Grateful. Optimistic. Very happy I accepted your proposition.'

'I meant physically.'

Ah. She flushed. She'd forgotten that this

weekend wasn't as momentous for him as it was for her. 'I ache,' she said, determinedly switching her focus from the intangible to the tangible. 'And I'm sore. But in a good way. I've discovered muscles—and stamina—I didn't know I had.'

'Do you hurt?'

'No.'

'Good.'

'How do *you* feel?' she asked, suddenly needing to know, apropos of the gap in momentousness, whether he found her inexperienced efforts a turn-on or tedious, whether she was just a pity project that appealed to his hero complex and he was simply going through the motions or whether he genuinely found her as irresistible as she found him.

He arched one dark eyebrow. 'Me?'

She nodded.

'Oh, I feel just fine,' he said with a slow seductive smile that, to her relief, suggested he didn't find her remotely tedious and really wasn't just going through the motions. 'In fact, come over here and I'll show you.'

CHAPTER EIGHT

LEO FELT SO FINE, so utterly content with the situation here, that when Sunday afternoon rolled around and he realised that one weekend wasn't going to be nearly enough, that he needed longer with Willow, it really was no big deal. It was simply that he wanted more of the stunningly inventive sex they'd been having, which was just as incredible as he'd anticipated, possibly even better.

That first time had been it for slow and careful. Having discovered what her body was capable of and newly empowered, Willow had embraced experimentation with an enthusiasm he could never have imagined. The ease and speed with which she picked up new skills was impressive. The brilliant wielding of pastels wasn't her hands' only talent, and the things she could do with her mouth… *Theos*.

She'd made him physically lose control, repeatedly, something he could not recall ever doing before, but despite his initial unease, he'd come to realise that it was no cause for concern. No one had been hurt and as far as he was aware the world had not ended, which why he was so comfortable with the idea of extending the weekend by a day or two.

After all, it wasn't as if he were planning on going AWOL for a month. He'd only be away from the office for forty-eight hours max. He'd been on business trips that lasted longer without any drama. Disaster was unlikely to strike in such a short time and if it did, he was always on end of a telephone. His staff, his clients, the board, *no one* need ever know what he was getting up to when not at his desk answering the occasional email. Assuming Willow was amenable, it was an excellent plan—personally and professionally speaking, the best of both worlds.

'I should go,' sighed the goddess in question, glancing at her watch and peeling herself off him with what encouragingly felt like reluctance.

Before she could get very far, however, Leo rolled her onto her back and pinned her to the bed. 'Do you want to?'

Her shimmering gaze met his, her breath

catching, the pulse at the base of her neck fluttering madly. She gave her head a minute shake, the colours of her hair warm in the early evening sun, and he was filled with an absurdly overwhelming relief at the knowledge that she wasn't done with this any more than he was. 'Not right now, no.'

'Then don't.'

Of course Willow was going to agree to stay. She didn't want to give any answer other than *yes, yes, yes*.

The thought of leaving Santorini and Leo had been the only sour note in an otherwise gorgeous weekend. She wasn't nearly ready to go. She was having far too brilliant a time. Not only had she discovered the wonders of great sex, she was also living the adventure and passion Selene had talked about and she'd so envied.

The private jet… The beautiful estate with its shimmering infinity pool and perfect curve of pebbled beach… The handsome, enigmatic billionaire who burned her clothes off every time he looked at her, who showed her fireworks and patience, whichever was required… Why would she want to give any of that up?

She had nothing pressing to return to. Work

on her next commission didn't start for a while. The handful of social engagements she had in the diary were easily cancellable and the neighbour who checked in on her father every other day reported he was fine.

She estimated she had around two weeks before reality struck and her world became one of pain, but she'd be long gone by then. No one had ever witnessed the trauma she went through when on her period and no one ever would. She was at her most vulnerable at such times, weak and a wreck. The thought of the emotional intimacy that having someone with her throughout would engender tightened her throat and curdled her stomach. Leo, with his three sisters, might claim to be unfazed by girls' stuff but even he would probably be thrown by it, and she wanted him to remember her as bright and strong, as a crazy, colourful moment in his otherwise ordered, controlled life.

So a week or so of playing Cinderella and pretending that she was easy-going and care-free, that her life wasn't ruled by endometriosis, was all she could have, but it was infinitely better than the nothing she'd been expecting.

'Tomorrow's Monday,' she said, nevertheless inordinately giddy at the prospect. 'Don't you have to work?'

'I don't need to be in the office to do that. I am certain I can remain here for another day or two without the company imploding.'

A day or two, no more? Hmm. That was a bit disappointing. It wouldn't be nearly enough for her, she suspected. But maybe she could deploy her new-found wiles to persuade him to reassess. He appeared to be in a changing-the-plan kind of a mood, after all, and with the high she was riding at the moment, anything felt possible.

'All right,' she said, smiling up into his dark gleaming eyes, excited at what the next forty-eight hours—hopefully more—might hold.

'Good.'

With the flash of a satisfied smile, Leo leapt off the bed and grabbed his phone. He made a series of calls, all of which were in Greek, none of which she understood. Then he sent for her belongings, which arrived the following morning, and that was the extent of communication with the outside world for a while.

Two days later, mid-morning, Leo's phone rang for what felt like the hundredth time of the day. He set the coffee maker on the lit stove so it could do its thing, then fished the device from the back pocket of his shorts. Zander's name scrolled across the screen. Resisting the temptation to simply cancel the call and get on with preparing breakfast in peace, Leo reminded himself that, however intrusive, he still had responsibilities, and pressed the green button that answered the call.

'So Leo,' drawled his brother, once they'd established that it was indeed a good, if late, morning. 'Where the hell are you and what exactly are you doing?'

'I'm on Santorini,' he drawled right back, reaching for the box that contained four fresh croissants, which he'd just been out to buy, and tipping them onto a plate. 'And I'm working from home.'

'So your assistant said. What I want to know is, why?'

'Why not?'

There was a pause, during which Leo headed to the fridge for the yogurt, and then came a faintly concerned, 'Are you ill?'

'I've never felt better. Why do you ask?'

'Because you haven't worked from home in years. Or ever, come to think of it.'

'As per your instructions,' he said, thinking of Willow still slumbering upstairs and recalling the recommendation Zander had made on the balcony of the hotel at which Daphne's wedding reception had taken place. 'I'm lightening up. While continuing to work. You seem to manage it.'

'Right. What's going on?'

'Nothing's going on,' he said as he tipped the yogurt into a bowl. 'What's going on with you?'

'You sound odd.'

'You sound confused.'

'I am. This isn't like you. When are you back?'

First thing tomorrow should have been Leo's answer, given that technically, all remained of his two-days-max weekend extension was this afternoon. Yet he couldn't seem to formulate the words. Because the truth was, he didn't want to have to return to reality just yet. He wanted to prolong his and Willow's Mediterranean island mini break even further, but now not solely to ensure a continuation of the sex.

There were things about her he was increasingly keen to know. Such as how she'd become an artist. Why she'd chosen those colours for her hair and what the multiple earrings and the nose stud were all about. He was interested in finding out about her hopes, her dreams, her fears. To remind himself—in case he should need reminding—of all the reasons why long term she was wrong for him, naturally.

Since they'd arrived on the island and embarked on a sex marathon, conversation had generally been sparse, impersonal and inconsequential. Over a light lunch by the pool yesterday, however, the morning having been taken up with more calls and emails than he'd appreciated, she'd quizzed him on the Stanhope Kallis empire. Somehow they'd ended up talking about his family dynamics, an exchange which had turned out to be anything but trivial.

'Why does it have to be you who does everything?' she'd asked, popping a *dolmades* into her mouth and making distractingly appreciative little sounds as she ate.

'What do you mean?' He'd selected an olive, tossed it in the air and caught it in his mouth, which had earned him a beaming smile and a brief round of applause.

'You have five siblings,' she'd then pointed out. 'You all work for the business in one capacity or another. You're all Selene's children and you're all now adults. You no longer have to be the one with all the responsibility.'

'No,' he'd had to admit, although, oddly, that had never occurred to him before. 'That's true. But it's a role that was always destined to be mine and I've been doing it for years. Giving up control is a hard habit to break.'

'You broke it for sex with me. You could break it for other things if you wanted to.'

Well, yes, he could, in *theory*, he'd supposed, but—'What I want is irrelevant.'

'I'd give anything to have someone to share the responsibility of a parent with,' she'd said before giving him an irritatingly knowing look and adding, 'I think you're a control freak.'

Leo had agreed. He was. With the suspicion that he shared too many regrettable genes with his mother and the brutal awareness that his success as CEO was down to sheer willpower rather than any innate talent, he had to be. And that was fine by him.

'There are worse things to be,' he'd said, wincing a little on the inside at the defensive note he could hear in his voice.

'There are better things to be, too.'

Not wanting to argue the point, he'd pulled her onto his lap then and that had been that for conversation for an hour. But her observations had nevertheless hit home. The responsibility he bore was crushing, relentless and draining, and he was sick of the endless firefighting.

What if he let his siblings deal with their mother for a change, should the need arise? he thought now while his poor, bewildered brother waited for an answer down the other end of the line. Surely together they could figure it out. He didn't *have* to be the one Daphne and the others always turned to for help. And why couldn't he delegate? Zander, his second in command—albeit hitherto in name only—was always on at him to loosen the reins. He'd be thrilled to take on more of the burden of the business, even temporarily.

In fact, he—Leo—could implement this new strategy this very minute. If he instructed his brother to take the helm for a while, he could remain on the island with Willow, who'd mentioned last night that she had a few weeks before she needed to travel to Italy to start her next commission, without the intrusion of emails and calls. Free from external demands, he could focus one hundred percent on getting to know the woman beneath the surface.

Zander was right. His current behaviour wasn't like him, but the last couple of days had proved that the plates carried on spinning even if he wasn't there to dash between the poles that held them up 24-7, and he hadn't had a break in years. He might never have ditched duty for pleasure before, but he wouldn't be leaving his ship without a captain. It was just that for, say, a few more days, that captain wouldn't be him.

There was no need to feel queasy about it.

Zander was extremely competent, and, possibly even more importantly, champing at the bit. He'd be able to handle all the different strands of the business that demanded the CEO's attention. He was tough enough to face Selene down in the event that was required.

And it wasn't as if he himself would somehow find himself in too deep with Willow along the way, even if such an eventuality was on the cards, which it was not. He had no appetite for the level of chaos that emotional commitment wrought, and she was very much not his idea of a life partner. If and when he did marry, it would be to someone like him, someone who wouldn't upend his existence and who wouldn't expect more from him than he was willing to give.

Opposites might attract but they didn't make for happiness. Just look at the example his parents had set. Their marriage had been a volatile train wreck, characterised by fiery yelling on his mother's part and an increasingly cold shoulder on his father's, although since they'd produced six children presumably they hadn't been in opposition all the time.

He wanted none of that. He'd choose an even-keeled union of mutual respect and companionship over passion and ice any day. *His* children weren't going to be subjected to snide comments in the common room. *They* weren't going to repeatedly lose friends through no fault of their own.

But he'd spent over a decade looking out for his family, and actually, now that he thought about it, what he wanted *wasn't* irrelevant. He deserved to think solely about himself for a change and deep down he yearned to kick up his heels and have some contained, harmless fun. Another change of plan was no particular cause for concern. It wasn't a whim. He knew what he wanted. And what he was doing. Everything would be fine.

'Are you still there?' said Zander with a sharpness that jolted him out of his thoughts and returned him to the conversation.

'Yes.'

'So?'

'I'm taking some personal time,' said Leo, switching off the stove beneath the now bubbling coffee pot.

'Some *what*?'

'Some days off. A break.'

'Now?'

'Yes.'

'For how long?'

'Not long. I'll keep you posted. In the meantime, from this moment on, you're in charge. You know what to do. No need to run anything past me. Just don't let me down.'

Before Zander could start asking more questions he was unable to answer, such as whether he'd completely lost his mind, Leo hung up and tossed the phone on the worktop. He located a tray and began loading it up, only to freeze when his skin started to prickle, an indication, he'd come to realise, that Willow was in the vicinity.

'Who was that?' she said, sidling into the kitchen wearing the black bikini and the pink silky robe that she'd sported the afternoon he'd met her and had caused him so many sleepless nights thereafter.

'That was Zander.'

'Trouble back in Athens?'

If there was trouble anywhere, it wasn't in Athens. It was right here in the seemingly unquenchable desire he had for her that was messing with his behaviour and turning his life upside down. 'Quite the opposite.'

'What do you mean?'

'Do you have anywhere else to be right now?'

She shook her glorious head. 'No.'

'Anything else to be doing?'

'No.'

'Well, as of this moment, for a few more days, at least, neither do I.'

'I don't understand,' she said with a faint frown. 'I thought we were leaving this evening.'

'I've put Zander in charge of the company for a while.'

The frown vanished. Her eyebrows shot up and her jaw dropped. 'Are you serious?'

'Yes.' He handed her the plate of croissants and the bowl of yogurt, which she automatically took.

'Why?'

'Because I,' he said, picking up the tray and heading out onto the patio while vaguely wondering why he wasn't more bothered about both handing over the company keys to Zander and the upheaval to his life Willow was causing, 'need a holiday.'

It took Willow the whole of breakfast to get over her shock at Leo's holiday announcement. She felt the hit of caffeine as it entered her bloodstream—impossible not to with the way he made coffee—but she barely tasted the deliciously buttery and flaky croissant or the soft creamy yogurt sweetened with lightly fragranced honey.

All she could think was, could *she* have

been behind his decision to take a break? Had her feminine wiles really worked their magic? Could their conversation over lunch yesterday have somehow made him reassess his relationship with responsibility and his siblings?

Whether they had or not, and realistically she knew that *not* was far more likely, it was ridiculous how pleased she was with this latest development in their affair. She didn't know why. It changed nothing. It proved nothing. Yet her heart was flipping about in her chest and she could hardly contain the smile that kept threatening to spread across her face, which was a concern because she didn't like to think what any of it might mean.

She had to be careful, she told herself sternly as Leo refilled her cup with rocket fuel. She mustn't make the mistake of thinking that what they were doing was anything other than temporary. Longer term with Leo was out of the question. Even if she could change her conflicting feelings about commitment and love—which seemed impossible when they ran so deep—sex aside, she was about as far removed from his usual type as it was possible to be. Lowering her guard and falling for him would be a one-way ticket to disappointment and despair. She had to live in, and make the most of, the present.

'What would you like to do today?' he asked, once again apparently able to read her mind.

Her body wanted to go back to bed with him because amazingly, despite all their efforts to assuage it, desire still burned within her, as hot as ever. But her head was thinking that perhaps it would help to get out of the house. The last few days, although glorious, had been nothing if not intense. It was little wonder she'd lost her sense of perspective. A return to the outside world might give her the dose of reality she needed to stay on track. Besides, with all the drawings of him she'd been producing, she needed to pick up a new sketchbook.

'Seeing as we're on holiday,' she said, confident that a change of scenery was all she required to keep her feet on the ground, 'and I haven't been abroad in a decade, I'd like to see the island.'

That afternoon, as he watched Willow pick her way around the limestone ruins of a settlement that dated back to the eleventh century B.C., Leo reflected that her proposal to explore had been an excellent one. The only reason he hadn't suggested it himself was because for the first time in years he hadn't been thinking with his brain.

In the absence of sex he'd been able to focus more efficiently on his plan to get the answers to the questions about her he had. Among myriad other tiny but oddly fascinating details he'd gleaned en route to the archaeological site of Ancient Thera via a coastal road that required the careful navigation of twenty-two hairpin bends, he'd discovered that she streaked her hair for no other reason than because she liked the colours. She'd bought the tiny diamond nose stud to celebrate her first sale and the earrings because, why not? And she lived and worked in London in a top floor light-filled studio that she'd bought with the money she'd inherited from her mother.

For an hour now they'd been wandering around the deserted remains of temples and houses with mosaic floors. The millennia-old graffiti were fascinating. The sea views were spectacular. His phone hadn't rung once, a novelty about which he wasn't sure he felt pleased or twitchy.

'I wish I'd brought my pastels with me,' said Willow, shading her eyes against the sun as she stood like a queen on a rock that was far too high and close to the edge of the cliff for his liking and gazed around at the rugged scenery from beneath her floppy-brimmed hat. 'The depth and intensity of the colours here could make even the most committed portraitist switch to landscapes.'

'Let me help you down.'

She took the hand he extended and beamed him a smile that was brighter than the sun, which, this being Greece in July, was saying something. 'Thank you.'

'How did you become an artist?' he asked, assuring himself that the intense relief he experienced at having removed her from potential harm was perfectly normal.

'I didn't have much of a choice. It's the only thing I can do. I left school with just one A level. In art.'

'Why was that?'

'Because of my condition, I missed a lot of classes. The exam timetable was not my friend.'

'Did no one ever notice?'

'My school had two thousand students,' she said dryly, as they retraced their steps down the path that led back to the ruined city and away from lethal four-hundred-metre drops. 'There were three hundred in my year. There wasn't a lot of one-on-one attention. Lots of people slipped through the cracks for a variety of reasons and I was simply one of them.'

Leo tried to imagine such a situation occurring at the top boarding school in England he'd attended from the ages of eight to eighteen and failed. 'Your father?'

'Grief-stricken. But it was fine,' she said with a quick, dismissive wave of her hand that made him wonder if it really had been. 'I was never going to be able to hold down a conventional job with the amount of sick leave I'd have to take, so I didn't need any qualifications anyway.'

'Did you go to art college?'

'No. I've done courses but I'm mostly self-taught. I built up a collection of work—while moonlighting as a waitress—and then basically blagged my way into exhibitions.'

'You're tenacious.'

'I've had to be,' she said with a wry twist of her mouth. 'I wasn't always successful, but luckily, people seem to like what I do. More to the point, *I* like what I do. My work is versatile and varied and fits in with other things and I love it. Not many people can claim that.'

'That's true.'

'Can you?' she said, darting him a quick, unsettlingly probing look as the remnants of the amphitheatre hove into view. 'Do you enjoy your job, Leo?'

Not particularly was the answer that broke free of its confines and clamoured to be heard. But he ignored it the way he did every time resentment at his fate reared its ugly, shameful head. There had never been any point in wondering what might have happened if he'd simply refused to leave university mid-course, turned his back on everything he'd been groomed for and pursued his dream of winning the America's Cup. He was CEO of one of the world's largest, most successful privately owned corporations. He had wealth and power. He had no right to envy others for being able to choose their own path. Envy was destructive and it was ridiculous to regret something that had never really been a possibility in the first place.

'I'm extremely good at it,' he said, oddly unable to lie to her outright when usually the words came smoothly.

'That doesn't answer the question.'

'Doesn't it?'

'Perhaps it does,' she said with a tiny nod of understanding. 'Duty is important to you.'

'My destiny was drummed into me at an early age.'

'What would you have done if you'd had the choice?'

'I've have sailed,' he said without a second's hesitation. 'Competitively.'

'Do you own a boat?'

'Not anymore.'

'That's a shame.'

'Why?'

'We could have taken it out tomorrow.'

While Leo stopped to inspect a pile of old stones at the edge of the amphitheatre, Willow sat on a rock and took her brand-new sketch-book out of her bag. After several annoyingly poor attempts to capture the dusty, ruined landscape that stretched out before her, she gave up and slipped on her sunglasses so that instead she could watch the man she was sleeping with, an infinitely more fascinating sight.

She had not missed the evasiveness with which he'd responded to her more probing questions as they'd wandered back along the path. Or the trace of resentment in his voice that she thought she'd caught, not for the first time.

What was the story there?

Because there definitely *was* one.

Since they'd met he'd indicated too many

times to count that, for him, duty trumped all else, and if he were comfortable with that then all well and good, but clearly, he wasn't. She had the feeling that he was doing a job he didn't really want. Like her, his life appeared to be limited by circumstances. Maybe, like her, he found the idea of changing those circumstances too great a risk to take.

The question, which was far too personal ever to be broached, of course, the answer to which she absolutely did not need to know, was, why?

CHAPTER NINE

WHY LEO HAD arranged for a yacht to be brought over to the villa overnight, so that he could take Willow out in the morning, he had no idea. He hadn't sailed for years. When the all-consuming nature of his new job had hit home in the aftermath of his father's death, he'd had to shut down his old life completely in order to be able to concentrate on maintaining the legacy.

But the hint of wistfulness that had woven through Willow's words when she'd asked him if he owned a boat to take out to sea had been answered by an unexpected yearning of his own, which had nagged away at him all the way back to the house until it had eventually occurred to him that one key point of a holiday, surely, was having the opportunity to do the things you didn't usually have time for.

The yacht was moored to a rarely used buoy in the cove. After breakfast, laden with bags and a cool box, he and Willow walked down to the jetty, where the tender was tethered. He stowed the kit and helped her aboard, then fastened her into a life jacket before donning his own.

Itching with the need to get his hands on the sheets and the wheel, to flex his toes against the smooth warm wood beneath his bare feet, Leo fired up the engine. Adrenalin pumped through him at the novel idea of spending all day at sea. His head filled with the memory of how much he'd once loved it, how much he'd relied on being able to get onto the water whenever he'd needed to escape his parents' volatile relationship as an angry teenager burning up with helplessness. And as they sped across the warm south Aegean waters towards the sleek white craft that was bobbing there, calling to him like a siren, the chaos of the last few days dissipated beneath a familiar, welcome blanket of calm.

Leo sailed them into a bay that was perfect for snorkelling and dropped anchor a hundred metres offshore. Willow had never snorkelled before so that was another thing he taught her to do.

Possibly, she didn't pay as much attention to the underwater paradise as she should have done, but then possibly there was no man on earth as compellingly attractive as him. The cool turquoise sea and brightly coloured fish that darted around them and through the rocks were no match for a set of strong shoulders, powerful thighs and a competency on and in water that she found irresistible.

She hadn't been able to take her eyes off him as he'd handled the boat. Apart from the anchor haulage mechanism, there was little other automation. This particular yacht was for working, not for relaxing on with a gin and tonic while computers, or a crew, did the rest.

And Lord, how he'd worked it.

The minute they'd climbed aboard Leo had switched into action. While she'd settled herself on a seat, aware that she'd be of little assistance, he'd leapt from deck to cockpit and back again, familiarising himself with the boat, he'd informed her, and conducting various checks of equipment. Once satisfied everything was in order, off they'd set, and from that moment on, he'd barely stood still, whether at the wheel, scanning the horizon, or responding to the flapping of the sail with an impressively masterful tack.

He might like to come across as icy cold and ruthlessly controlled—although, come to think of it, she hadn't seen that side to him for a while now—but he obviously had a passion for sailing. He'd hardly stopped grinning all morning and he was more relaxed than she'd ever have imagined him capable of being.

She couldn't help but wonder if *this* time, they really were where they were because of something she'd said, and that, as much as the raw physicality and sheer strength which was on display, warmed her in a way that had nothing to do with the sun drying her off as she lay stretched out on the foredeck beside Leo, who was sitting with his elbows resting on his drawn-up knees and staring at the horizon.

'Thank you for arranging this,' she murmured, lethargic after all the snorkelling which had been followed by lunch, her head resting on her folded arms, eyes half-closed.

'You're welcome. It's been good to stand behind the wheel again.'

'I can't imagine a gentle meander along the Santorini coast is quite the same as hurtling across the Atlantic in gale force winds.'

'No,' he agreed, reaching into the cool box for the two remaining ice-cold bottles of beer and popping the caps off. 'But it doesn't matter. The wind in your hair and the spray on your face is exhilarating whatever body of water you're on and whatever the weather. And anywhere there's an unobstructed horizon gives you the freedom of being able to head in any direction you choose.'

Was he aware how wistful he sounded? Was he only talking about sailing? Willow shifted onto her side, partly to take the bottle he handed her but mainly so she could see his expression more clearly. 'It might have been a while, but you seem very at ease on board.'

'I've been sailing ever since I could walk.'

'So why did you give it up?'

'I had to. I had no choice.'

But had he? Really? She got that he'd had to abandon the idea of competition when he took over the company, but couldn't he have continued to do it for fun?

She shouldn't probe. A tiny muscle flickered in his jaw and it was none of her business. And yet the questions had been niggling away at her ever since they'd left Ancient Thera the day before and they had to talk about *something*. Conversation wasn't dangerous. It needn't lead to unwanted intimacy of the emotional kind. She was just curious as to what made him tick, that was all. It wasn't as if she'd be giving any of her own secrets away.

'Why is duty so important to you?'

Leo lifted his bottle and took a mouthful of beer before answering, as if needing the fortification before replying. 'My father wasn't the easiest of men,' he said eventually, with a wry twist of his lips. 'He was weak when it came to my mother, which I didn't realise until I was older, and he could be cold and aloof, but he spent a lot of time with me, discussing the business, when I was a kid. He regularly took me with him to the offices in London and Athens. I remember repeatedly being introduced as the next boss and although it was always said in a joking kind of a way everyone knew he was deadly serious.'

'Did he never consider anyone else?'

He shook his head. 'He came from the sort of family where the eldest son automatically inherits.'

'That must have put you under a lot of pressure.'

'There was never any question or discussion about it,' he said, interestingly neither confirming nor denying her observation. 'It was always presented as a fait accompli.'

'No wonder you're resentful.'

He cast her a quick, sharp glance. 'Resentful?'

'Occasionally it comes through when you're

talking about your family,' she said. 'And it's completely understandable. I mean, you were so young. As you once told me, the learning curve was steep. You must have had to make many personal sacrifices along the way.'

'None that I wasn't willing to make,' he said with a shrug that was perhaps a little too sharp to be casual. 'I had to give it everything. I couldn't let him down. In business, he demanded and commanded respect and I had that for him in spades. Within five years of merging the two companies, he doubled the bottom line. He halved staff turnover. Professionally speaking, his shoes were always going to be big ones to fill.'

'But you do fill them, don't you?'

'I do. I more than fill them. But they don't fit very well.'

'Whatever do you mean by that?'

Despite the intensity of the midday sun Leo's blood chilled when he realised he'd just revealed more than he'd meant to. Why had he done that? Had the heat gone to his head? Had too much time under water this morning reduced the oxygen supply to his brain? Was he drunk? Or had he simply been thrown by the discovery that if Willow had noticed his resentment he wasn't as good at keeping a lid on his emotions as he'd always assumed?

Something had to account for the slip, but whatever it was, it wouldn't happen again. The thrill of being back on board and out to sea had obliterated his caution. The blanket of calm had given him a false sense of security. Unwisely, he'd relaxed and then he'd lowered his guard.

But all he had to do to correct the situation was raise it, and that was what he'd do because he could not afford to let the unsettlingly perceptive Willow and the chaos she carried with her get under his skin. This raging affair of theirs was a purely temporary arrangement. It was not in any way even-keeled and cool, so she was not, and never would be, the one for him.

'Nothing in particular,' he said, sliding his gaze from hers back to the horizon and ignoring the shaft of what felt strangely like disappointment that struck him in the chest.

'You're being evasive again.'

'And you're being nosy.'

'I'm just curious about the man I've been sleeping with for five days,' she said with a lightness he sensed was deceptive. 'I've answered all your questions. You have a habit of avoiding mine. It makes me wonder what you have to hide.'

'I have nothing to hide.' Just things he didn't intend to share with someone like her. Or with anyone ever, in fact.

'Prove it.'

'I don't need to prove anything.'

'Then humour me.'

'I don't need to do that either.'

He glanced her way in time to see a triumphant spark light her eyes. 'So you *are* hiding something.'

The only things he was hiding were intense irritation at being tied in knots and a rapidly growing concern about the torrent of words on the subject that were piling up in his head, demanding release. What that was about he hadn't a clue. He had no intention of spilling his guts, which would render him exposed, vulnerable and weak. He had never sought understanding or sympathy, and he didn't want them either, least of all from a potentially destructive force like Willow. He didn't know why he'd started talking about his relationship with his father in this way in the first place. He never had done before, not even with his siblings.

But she was looking at him as if trying to peer into his soul and he couldn't seem to tear his gaze away, no matter how hard he tried. The longer it went on, the greater the trembling of his defences and the less he could remember why he kept his cards close to his chest. Her gaze was shimmering, bottomless and as he lost himself in it, he had the disturbing feeling that his guard wasn't just down; he didn't even know where it was.

'Fine,' he found himself saying, unease drumming through his veins as his protective shield lay shattered about him and the words poured out. 'I might be good at it but the role doesn't come easily to me. I don't thrive under pressure. I don't enjoy zigzagging continents and endlessly crossing time zones. I find the responsibility of employing tens of thousands of staff an unbearable weight and the awareness that if I'm not extremely vigilant everything for which I'm responsible will come crashing down pervades my every waking moment.'

For a moment Willow didn't respond. When she did it was with a slightly stunned, 'Wow.'

'You did ask.'

'That is *not* the image you present.'

Thank God. 'Of course it isn't.'

'Is that why you're so big on control?'

'Yes. It's got me through some tough times.' His father's death... Inheriting the business...

His sister's illness… He didn't know how he'd have coped without it.

'I thought it was because you feared you were too like your mother.'

'There's that, too,' he admitted, now that he'd started apparently unable to stop. 'She is wild and self-centred and people can sometimes get hurt by her thoughtlessness. Not only do I share her genes, in my teenage years, I had also had a tendency to behave like that sometimes.'

'The boat you crashed?'

'I'd just discovered in the press that she was having an affair with my then best friend's father.'

'That must have been awful.'

It had been worse than awful. It had unleashed a storm of hurt and embarrassment, frustration and fury that he hadn't know how to handle. 'It wasn't just the once,' he said, ignoring the memories trying to muscle their way into his head. 'I lost count of the number of friends I made and lost. The boat belonged to her. I took it out on my own one morning in the summer holidays and drove onto the rocks. I was sixteen. I was angry. It worked. I'm not angry anymore.'

'Are you sure about that?'

'Absolutely,' he said, with a sharp nod of his head and a mouthful of beer.

It was about the only thing he was certain of at the moment. The crash, unplanned, instinctive, had shaken him up badly. In the aftermath of his rescue, he'd been told by his father—not that he'd needed a lecture, having realised it on his own—that his increasingly reckless behaviour wasn't acceptable. He hadn't been willing to give up sailing just then, so he'd decided to give up emotion. If he allowed nothing to affect him, he wouldn't have the urge to react. There'd be no further loss of control, no more damage. Simple.

'It would be understandable if you were.'

'It would. However, I'm not. I find my mother frustrating and exhausting, but that's it.'

'Right,' she said dryly, with a nod that suggested she knew something he didn't and made him feel as though the deck upon which he was sitting were made of jagged glass shards.

'What?' he muttered eventually, unable to stand the scrutiny and the knowingness any longer.

'You have such a lot going on in that handsome head of yours.'

He did. And he had to keep it all in there. Enough of the soul searching and sharing. It was wholly unnecessary. He hadn't spent years denying his emotions only to let them loose in response to one pertinent question. He would put a stop to this sightseeing nonsense. He and Willow weren't a couple. Bed was where they functioned best and it was ridiculous to have indulged her otherwise. He'd only put her in the driving seat for the first two days they'd been on the island, but somehow she was still in it and it couldn't continue.

'Can you tell what I'm thinking right now?' he said, putting their now empty bottles back in the cool box and closing the lid with a snap.

Her gaze dipped to his mouth and lingered. 'That a siesta in the cabin would be a good idea?'

'No,' he replied, resisting the temptation she presented because to take her down below when he was so on edge, his self-control un-nervingly shaky, would be mad, bad and incredibly dangerous. 'What I'm thinking is, it's time to go back.'

Leo wasn't the only one with a lot going on in his head. His confession occupied Willow's thoughts for every one of the nautical miles that sped by.

How on earth had he coped with the stress

of doing a job he didn't feel equipped for all these years? The internal struggles he'd had to have faced, the tough decisions he'd had to have made... She couldn't imagine it, although she did now understand his need for control and order and his desire for privacy.

The suppression of his true self to get the job done and protect others, however, didn't sound very healthy at all. But then who was she to judge? She was hardly a model of rational thinking. She was avoiding the operations she'd been told would help alleviate the symptoms of her endometriosis because of a fear that she knew logically was unlikely to materialise. She was as trapped by events of the past as he was.

It was a shame he'd put an end to the day because she'd been having a fabulous time, but she got it, just as she got why the smiles had vanished and Leo was now tight-jawed and anything but relaxed at the wheel. She'd prodded him into talking when he hadn't wanted to and he wasn't happy about it.

So she'd back off and give him some breathing space, the way he'd done for her when she'd needed it. It would be no bad thing for her either, come to think of it. Because now she'd had a glimpse of the man beneath the facade she wanted to know more. She wanted to know everything, which was not an option, so she could do with some time alone to shore up her defences against the threat to the emotional distance she was determined to maintain.

'What's the plan for tomorrow?' she asked once they'd made it back to the villa, needing to know so she could figure out how to get out of it.

'There isn't one,' came the blunt reply, which meant, she thought with some relief, that she could make her own.

Leo woke up gritty-eyed and grouchy, too unsettled by the events of the day before to have slept well. His dreams had been fractured and disturbing. The one in which he'd stretched out on a couch, his head in Willow's lap, and told her everything while she gently stroked his hair and murmured soothingly at regular intervals had been particularly alarming.

Discovering that he was alone in the bed didn't help his mood at all. Where was she? Had the brooding sullenness into which he'd descended yesterday afternoon driven her away once again? Had she had enough of the monosyllabic grunting that he'd been reduced to, left in the dead of night and gone back home? At

the thought of it, something unpleasant slithered into his stomach, until she emerged from
the bathroom in a towel and a cloud of rose-
scented steam, at which point it slithered right
back out again.

'Good morning,' he said, his voice gruff with
sleep, although other parts of his anatomy were
rapidly waking up.

'Good morning,' she replied absently, reaching for her clothes.

She ditched the towel, which gave him hope,
but then she started dressing, which dashed it.
Sightseeing might be no longer an option, but
he hadn't put a stop to anything else.

'What are you doing?'

'Getting dressed.'

'I can see that.' He frowned. 'But why?'

'Because my taxi will be here any minute.'

Leo sat bolt upright, fully awake now, his
pulse pounding and his mind racing. What the
hell? She *was* leaving? 'Where are you going?'

'I thought I'd start with the Three Bells of
Fira,' she said, fluffing out her glorious hair
then pushing her sunglasses into it. 'And see
what I felt like doing after that.'

He blinked. Shook his head to clear it.
'What?'

'I'm going sightseeing,' she said. 'I told you

I wanted to see more of the island. So that's
what I'm going to do.'

'On your own?'

'Yes.'

'I'll join you,' he said, flinging back the
sheet and swinging his legs round to surge
to his feet.

'There's no need for that,' she countered,
alarm flickering across her face as he pulled
on his shorts and grabbed a T-shirt. 'We're not
joined at the hip.'

There was every need for that. Forget his
decision of yesterday to confine them to the
villa. He wasn't having her wandering around
the place on her own. What if something happened to her? It didn't bear thinking about. She
was a guest in his home. She was his responsibility. And that was all there was to it.

While she slipped her feet into flats, he
racked his brains for arguments to convince
her to see things his way. 'You don't speak the
language.'

'I have an app. I'll manage.'

'You don't know where you're going. You
could be taken for a ride.'

'That's a risk I'm willing to take.'

'I'd *like* to join you.'

'Well, *I'd* like some space,' she said, picking up her bag and dropping her phone into it, her smile small, the gaze that met his cool. 'So I'll see you later.'

The taxi dropped Willow off at the famous church known for its blue dome, its spectacular views and obviously, its three bells some time later, and she spent an hour exploring first it and then the streets around. Delightful and interesting though the experience was, however, it didn't give her the respite she'd been hoping for.

She'd been looking forward to spending some time alone. To cleansing her head and clarifying her thoughts and ridding herself of the longing to find out more about Leo. She had *not* anticipated missing him. Yet she did. She kept thinking of things to tell him. Time after time she turned to do so, expecting to find his tall broad frame in the vicinity, and without fail, a stab of disappointment at the realisation it wasn't struck her right through the heart.

It was ridiculous. After all, she was well accustomed to doing things on her own. With a largely absent father, both emotionally and physically, and no boyfriend to snuggle up with on the sofa, she'd been doing so for years. Somehow, though, probably because of the amount of time she'd spent with him, she'd got used to Leo's company. She'd had a glimpse of what it could be like to be part of a couple, and even though she knew it wasn't real, even though she'd be foolish to dwell on such things, secretly she'd found it thrilling.

She finished off the sparkling water she'd ordered at the cafe at which she'd stopped to escape the heat of the sun, her head teeming with exciting, possibly unwise yet unstoppable thoughts. Surely there'd be no harm in letting him tag along on her days out if he wanted to. As long as she remembered that they *weren't* a couple, that this fling of theirs had to come to an end—and soon, because time was marching—she'd keep her head. She was in no danger of falling for him. Nothing had changed in that regard. Her heart was still safely locked away and there it would stay.

'Meet me at the bottom of the Karavolades Stairs in half an hour,' she told him over the phone, blocking out the faint warning voice ringing in her head as she dropped some coins into the saucer that contained the bill and got to her feet, 'and I'll buy you lunch.'

Leo had spent the morning prowling around the villa, wondering what Willow was doing

and whether she was all right. He should have
gone after her was the thought that kept zip-
ping through his head. If his common sense
hadn't kicked in at the last minute to remind
him that he had to respect her request for space,
he would have.

He should also have been delighted with
the solitude her departure had generated. She
wasn't the only one who'd wanted it. Time
on his own suited his need to regroup and re-
build his defences perfectly. But the villa felt
strangely empty and colourless without her in
it. He'd got used to having her, her hair and her
jewellery around. To his bafflement, he wasn't
grateful she'd gone; he was annoyed.

His phone rang twice, but when he saw that
the callers weren't her but firstly Daphne, who
must have just returned from honeymoon, and
secondly, Zander, he ignored it. Within moments of hanging up on the third call, however,
he was out the door and on his way. The Karavolades Stairs, comprising over five hundred
steps, were steep and winding and plagued with
donkeys. Had Willow taken a hat to protect her
from the intense sun? And what shoes had she
been wearing? There was no handrail and the
stone could be deceptively slippery.

He didn't stop to think about the probing per-

sonal questions that might arise during lunch
and beyond. He didn't stop to analyse the absurd pleasure and sheer relief he felt at her invitation to join her. He just got in the car and
drove.

CHAPTER TEN

IN THE DAYS that followed, Leo took Willow to the hot springs on the tiny, uninhabited islet of Palea Kameni and the black sands of Kamari Beach. He introduced her to fragrant *souvlaki* and the sweet, creamy, custard-flavoured delights of *galaktoboureko*. One evening at an open-air cinema, they saw a film in Greek, which she didn't understand. He leaned in close to provide a continual translation, but his proximity had such a disastrous effect on her concentration that she didn't follow much of that either.

At no point did Willow regret having invited him to join her for lunch and the sightseeing that came after. Every time she turned to talk to him, there he was, and she felt no stab of disappointment, just a little leap of delight. Thankfully his surliness had gone. In fact, he'd become positively chatty. He'd told her more about his siblings and his relationship with each of his parents. About the sailing competitions he'd participated in as a youth and his job as an adult. By sticking to her modus operandi of getting other people to talk—he wasn't a client she was painting, but the principle was helpful—Willow had actually got away with sharing very little.

Tonight, he'd brought her to a tiny but packed taverna. It sat right over the bay, the wide pergola-covered terrace just a few metres up from the crystal-clear azure shallows. The colour of the painted wooden balustrade around the edge and the tables and chairs matched the cerulean sky. The setting sun radiated off the blinding white walls of the restaurant behind and hot pink bougainvillea trailed down the pergola uprights.

It was rustic and charming. The clientele was laid back, the conversation buzzed and not so long ago she'd have been surprised by the choice. She'd have imagined that a billionaire CEO with control issues and a liking for order might prefer a more formal setting in which to dine. But recently she'd seen less of that man and more of the one she felt he must have been before.

They were shown to a table in the corner,

overlooking the sea. It was too small really, and the positioning of the chairs—ideal for maximum appreciation of the view—resulted in a seating arrangement that was far too intimate for two people who were engaged in nothing more than an ultra-short affair. But Leo didn't steer her to another and she certainly wasn't going to object. She'd take all the close contact she could get.

He pulled out a chair for her and she sat down. He took the other and folded his large frame into it. When his knee bumped against hers beneath the table, a thousand volts shot though her. His scent dizzied her head. His proximity made her want to lean in to him and sigh.

Instead, she stayed where she was and picked up the menu. Understanding not a word of it, she put it back down. 'Would you order for me?'

'What would you like?'

She'd like to able to appreciate the romance of the place and the tangerine sunset, to gaze into his eyes and hold his hand. She'd like to burrow into his soul and stay there until she knew everything there was to know about him. She'd like to be able to share with him all her hopes and dreams, her insecurities and her fears, the hallmarks, she felt, of a proper relationship. To be able to overcome the emotional and physical obstacles that littered her life, to be his type and for things *not* to be coming to an end. But unfortunately none of that was on the menu, either in Greek or in English.

'What comes recommended?'

'The calamari is reputed to be excellent.'

'Then I'd like that.'

But unbeknownst to her, Willow had been on borrowed time and the idyll was about to implode. She was lying by the pool the following afternoon when a familiar stabbing sensation suddenly skewered her abdomen. For a moment she lay there, staring up the wisps of cloud streaking the sky like candyfloss, a little confused, a little alarmed, her heart beating a fraction too fast.

No.

This couldn't be happening.

She'd never been very regular, but it was way too soon, surely. It had to be indigestion or something.

What date was it anyway?

With a wince and a sickeningly familiar turn of her stomach, she reached for her phone. She brought up the calendar and responded with a jolt to the details on the screen. The twelfth? She'd been here for ten days already? How had that happened? She was only supposed to have stayed a week.

It wasn't hard to figure out why she'd lost track of time when she'd been so wrapped up in what she and Leo had been doing, but even so she ought to have had a few more days in hand. That was why she'd attributed her bloating to fine food and even finer wine and her extreme fatigue to a simple lack of sleep thanks to their burning the candle at both ends.

But how she'd missed such obvious signals when she'd had over eleven years of this, month in, month out, didn't matter. An analysis of the situation would have to wait. What was important was that she react. Fast. Because she couldn't let Leo see her go through what was about to happen. It would be brutal. Emotional and intimate. She would not appear weak and vulnerable in front of him. And what if he wanted to help? *God.* She'd have not a shred of dignity left.

Willow ignored the hot surge of emotion that suddenly rushed through her system in response to the sodding unfairness of life, and determinedly blinked back the unexpected sting of tears while cursing the hormones behind both. She'd always known their affair had an end date. She'd had a great time while it had lasted. It had been everything he'd promised and everything she'd hoped for, but now it was over. Instead of wallowing in regret and disappointment, she had to focus on getting away from Leo before the lovely bubble they'd created burst and things got very real indeed. So she got up off the sun lounger, gathered together her things and headed inside.

She was throwing her clothes into the suitcase that was lying open on the bed and determinedly ignoring the faint gnawing ache that she knew would soon intensify when Leo eventually found her.

'What on earth are you doing?' he asked, stock still in the doorway, a freshly made margarita in each hand.

The surprise she could hear in his voice bounced right off her. She resisted the temptation to ditch the suitcase and beg him to hold her close and kiss away the pain. She didn't stop for even a second. 'I have to go.'

'Why?'

'This has been fun but it's over.'

Out of the corner of her eye, she saw him set the drinks on top of a chest of drawers, a deep frown creasing his brow. 'What's going on, Willow?'

'Nothing's going on,' she said, plucking the pink silk robe off the armchair with clammy, trembling fingers and adding it to the pile. 'It's just that I need to leave.'

'You're very pale. Something's obviously wrong.'

He headed in her direction, his expression filled with concern she shouldn't—*didn't*—want. She made for the en suite bathroom before he could reach her, take her in his arms and pulverise her resolve. He was too much. Too perceptive. He was also not going to let this lie, she realised as she scooped up her toiletries and dropped them in her wash bag. There was nothing for it but honesty.

'I've started cramping,' she said, avoiding his penetrating gaze as she returned to the room. 'My pelvis aches. My period is imminent.'

'And?'

'It's going to be horrible. I turn into a soggy miserable wreck. You do not want to see me in that sort of a state. *I* don't want you to see me like that. So I'm going. Now.'

'Where?'

She dropped the wash bag into the suitcase, wishing she were better prepared, never more regretting that she hadn't kept a closer eye on the date. 'I need to get some supplies and then find a hotel.'

'Who will be there to take care of you?'

'No one,' she said, ignoring the brief twist of her heart and shoving everything down hard so it might fit. 'But I'm used to that. I can take care of myself.'

Leo folded his arms across his chest, his jaw set, his brow still furrowed, a stance that unfortunately suggested obstinacy and purpose. 'Who will rub your back and run you a bath?'

'I'll be fine,' she said with some obstinacy and purpose of her own. 'I always am.'

'Stay here and I can do both.'

For a split second, Willow allowed herself to imagine it because it sounded so wonderful. And then she thought of her dignity and the risk to the mile-high walls around her heart, at which point it very much didn't.

She gave her head a sharp shake and stifled the rogue pang of longing. 'No,' she said flatly as she zipped up one half of the case. 'It's too personal. Too embarrassing. I'd probably throw up on you and no one needs that.'

'You don't have to do this on your own,' he said, frustratingly persistent. 'Not this month, at least. Tell me what I can do to help and I will do it. I will make sure you have whatever you need.'

'You still want to solve my problems.'

'I don't like seeing people I care about suffering.'

She went very still, her heart giving a quick lurch, her gaze darting to his. She straightened and stared at him, packing momentarily forgotten. 'You care about me?'

'I'm sleeping with you. I'm sightseeing with you. Of course I do.'

She frowned. 'I see.'

'Is wanting to help you such a bad thing?' he asked with an assessing tilt of his head.

'It's a very bad thing.' The helping, the caring, the knowing that if she had this month she might crave another, and another... None of it was good.

'Why?'

'I don't want a knight in shining armour,' she said as much to remind herself of the fact as inform him of it. 'I never have. If I stay here, you'll see me at my worst. If I let you close enough to rub my back and run me baths, I may forget that this fling of ours was only ever supposed to be temporary, and that simply can't happen.'

'Why not?'

She had to tell him. She had to make him see that she could not and would not indulge his hero complex this time. 'When my mother died, my world fell apart, but I gradually put it back together again. My father didn't. He loved her so much that losing her has virtually destroyed him. He doesn't live. He just exists. He's not there for me. Or anyone. I will not put myself in that position. I will not put anyone else in that position should something happen to me. That's why not.'

'I am not going to fall in love with you.'

Her chest tightened for the briefest of seconds. 'Are you sure about that?'

He nodded. 'Quite sure.'

'Because I'm nothing like the type you usually go for.'

'It's not just that,' he said. 'I've seen how destructive love and the lack of control that goes with it can be and the chaos that can cause. I won't allow it to happen to me. I won't be that weak.'

She wished she had his confidence. 'But I might fall in love with you.'

For a moment he didn't respond. The frown deepened. A muscle hammered in his jaw. 'All right,' he said decisively, clearly having given that unwelcome thought due consideration. 'I won't rub your back or run you baths. I won't come anywhere near you if that's what you want. But give me a list and I will get what you need. I can feed you. Bring you drinks. What I *can't* do is let you walk out of another of my properties alone and in pain. That simply isn't the man I either am or want to be.'

'This isn't about you. It's about me.'

'You don't *really* want to go to a hotel, do you?'

An image floated into her head of her in some small, unfamiliar room, alone, again, robbed of the positivity she fought so hard to maintain, and the ache that throbbed in the pit of her stomach—now more emotional than physical—was so powerful it vaporised her inhibitions. 'No,' she admitted on a sigh.

'So take one of the spare rooms,' he said, un-surprisingly seizing advantage of the vulner-ability she'd exposed by her confession. 'Keep the door closed. Message me if and when you need something. You will barely notice I'm here.'

Willow's defences, weakened by the pain, the demoralising knowledge of what was to come and the yearning she was struggling to keep suppressed, were no match for such persua-sive arguments. Deep down she didn't want to have to go anywhere. She longed to be looked after, just once, and here Leo was offering her his support.

He was strong enough to handle the days to come, surely. She wouldn't make the mistake of thinking his assistance was anything more than it was. She'd be too preoccupied with managing the pain behind a closed door to think of anything. And when it was over, she would leave and she'd never have to see him again, which was just how it had to be.

'Are you going to counter-argue my every point?' she asked as the last of her resistance crumbled and she gave in to the inevitable.

'Yes,' he said, proving it with the faintest of smiles.

'Fine.'

Five long days later, nursing a large whisky, Leo sat on the terrace and stared out into the dark, warm, quiet night. Lights twinkled in the distance. Waves lapped gently at the beach below. In marked contrast to the peace and tranquillity of his surroundings, his head pounded and his stomach churned.

When he'd offered Willow his services, the thought of her being alone and in pain unbearable, the need to keep her close too fierce to deny, he had not imagined the depth of her suffering. He didn't think he'd ever forget the sight of her doubled up in agony or curled into a ball in the centre of the bed. It had been unexpectedly harrowing. How she dealt with it, month after month, on her own, he had no idea. She was unbelievably tough, but the mental toll had to be immense. He'd experienced a mere five days of it, on and off, as an occasionally useful bystander, and that was bad enough.

He hadn't enjoyed seeing her vibrancy diminished, her light out. Her distress had struck him square in the chest. No one deserved to live with that degree of discomfort and at one point, when she'd been feeling well enough to come downstairs for a couple of hours, he'd asked her if there wasn't anything she could do to alleviate her symptoms.

'The contraceptive pill would make things more manageable,' she'd told him, 'and God, it would be good to have a reliable time frame to work with, but it's possible it contributed to the arterial blood clot that my mother went into hospital to have removed. I just can't bring myself to take it and expose myself to the same sort of risk. It was supposed to be a simple operation, but she had a bad reaction to the anaesthetic and that was it.'

'What about surgery?' he'd asked, completely understanding the influence of the past on the present.

'I've also been told that in my case—which is mild even though the pain is excruciating—that would lessen the symptoms considerably. It would also increase the chances of having a family, which I'd like at some point, so on paper it's a no-brainer. But the thought of an anaesthetic terrifies me. What if I too go to sleep and never wake up? What would that do to my father? Look.' She'd held out a trembling hand. 'Even the mention of one makes me panic. And it's not just one operation. It could be many.'

Leo had taken her hand in his and held it until it had stopped shaking, itching to research the hell out of anaesthesia and then promise her the best medical treatment money could buy. Was there anything he could do to encourage her to have the surgery? he wondered now, turning his glass in his fingers as he continued to stare out into the distance. Her fears had to run very deep for her to favour the pain.

His phone beeped to indicate the arrival of a message and he knocked back the rest of the whisky before picking the device up. The text was from Zander.

Now I can see why you were so keen to take a holiday.

He frowned, set the glass down, then typed back.

What do you mean?

His brother's reply came in the form of a link, which had apparently been forwarded to him by their sister Thalia and came with the instruction not to shoot the messenger.

Trepidatiously, his heart thudding, Leo clicked on it. It took him to a page that purported to belong to a global magazine with an inclination for celebrity gossip. The subject of that page was him. Or more specifically, him and Willow.

Despite the enveloping warmth of the night, his blood chilled and his skin tightened as he scrolled down and read the article. The accompanying crystal-clear photos showed the two of them on the yacht the day they'd taken it out, snorkelling, jumping into the sea, talking on the deck, and more from the steep steps, the hot springs and the taverna.

Five stomach-churning minutes later, during which he'd sought and found a dozen similar sites with the same photos and the sort of headlines that came with exclamation marks, his vision was blurring and his chest was tight. How had it happened? was the question ricocheting around his brain as nausea rose up inside him. Why hadn't he noticed the cameras?

Everyone else, however, seemed to want to know, Who was she? Had Europe's most eligible, most elusive bachelor finally found love? If anyone had information about the mystery woman with the colourful hair and multiple piercings, they should click here.

The speculation was hideous. The invasion of his fiercely guarded privacy, and hers, boiled his blood. They were fodder for gossip—his mother's racy past had also been raked up yet again—and it was everything he'd sought to avoid. Only this time, *he* was the one at fault. No one else was to blame. He'd got so used to Willow's striking looks he'd forgotten that they did not fade into the background. He'd lost all sense of perspective. He'd been recklessly careless. He hadn't once considered the fact that he had an image of strength, of control and zero vulnerability to maintain and a business and a family to protect.

How could he have been so weak?

What the hell had he been *doing* all this time?

It wasn't remotely his responsibility to fix her issues but that hadn't stopped him. He *had* got a kick out of showing her sex could be good for her. That first time, here on the island, when she'd laughed with such abandon, such joy, he'd felt like he could rule the world. Ever since then, he'd behaved rashly—asking her to stay, putting Zander in charge of the company and then playing at being a couple as they did the tourist thing. When they'd talked—he, now he thought it, frequently without any filter at all— he'd listened closely to what she said. Her observations had made him question things he'd always accepted as fact. She'd developed unprecedented influence over him and he hadn't even noticed.

As to the reason he'd decided he had to play nurse these last few days, he was at a complete loss. It was yet another example of spontaneous, ill-advised decision-making. He'd been under no obligation to help. As she'd told him, she was used to handling it on her own. He had no business wishing he could take away her pain by absorbing it himself. How she managed her health was none of his concern and the giddy pleasure he'd felt when she'd sent him a message asking him to run her a bath and rub her back, which indicated a level of trust he'd hoped for but never expected, was as unwarranted as it was unwelcome.

Little by little, day by day, he'd been falling further and further under her spell, he realised, a cold sweat breaking out all over his skin. At some point, the nose stud, the earrings and the hair had stopped offending him. Now he couldn't—and didn't want to—imagine her any other way. She was perfect, just as she was, and that was not good, although his heart was thundering in his chest, in his head, in every inch of his body so loudly he couldn't quite remember why.

His phone beeped again, and he snatched it up, his hands shaking, the wariness winding through him intensifying to an almost unbearable degree.

Just as well I was able to rescue the merger, huh?!

Rescue the merger? What merger? Ah. Right. *That* merger. The one he'd flown to New York to arrange. The one that would add billions to the company's bottom line yet had not crossed his mind in days. What the hell had gone wrong with it? And when was the last time he'd even *thought* about the company? he wondered, his lungs constricting so much that breathing was suddenly difficult. When had he stopped worrying about how Zander was doing at the helm? How could he have abandoned his principles, the values with which he'd lived his life for over a decade, so easily?

He was completely out of control. Plates could come crashing down at any minute. It had to stop. All of it. Before his head was turned even further and he found himself entirely in Willow's thrall. Before he became someone he didn't want to be, ruled by emotion and selfishness, a slave to passion and ice and volatility. He had to claw back what was left of the life he knew and needed before it was destroyed for ever. Willow was back on her feet. The holiday was over. They were done.

Contrary to Willow's expectations, she hadn't been in too much pain to notice how magnificent Leo had been. He'd done exactly what he'd promised. He'd been patience and support personified, a tower of strength, and completely unfazed when she had thrown up on him, as she'd warned.

And now she was out the other side, staring up at the ceiling in the dark, the tumbling thoughts teeming through her head rendering sleep frustratingly elusive, she could see that everything she'd feared could all too easily come to pass. He was complex and intriguing, thoughtful and gorgeous, and her feelings for him were becoming dangerous.

Despite her best efforts to prevent it, she suspected she'd already invested herself emotionally in him. Why would she have caved in and requested the bath and the back rub if she didn't trust him? She wanted to tell him to ditch the job and buy a boat and support him through it. She wanted to take Selene by the shoulders and give her good shake along with an instruction to grow up. She found herself thinking ahead to next month and wishing she could have him by her side.

But that could never be. If she stuck around any longer those unwise feelings could all too easily deepen and she simply couldn't risk it. What if she allowed herself to love him and something happened to him? She'd be destroyed. And what if, despite his certainty that it would not happen, he developed feelings for her? He claimed to care about her. He'd seen her at her worst and hadn't run for the hills. It was possible he wasn't as impervious to love as he believed, and if he succumbed to the emotions he denied then *he* might be destroyed.

She deeply regretted not being stronger and clinging on to her resistance. She should never have been swayed by his arguments. If she wasn't careful she could be in so much trouble. The potential for heartbreak was immense and unacceptable. But it wasn't too late to rectify the situation. All she had to do was terminate their affair. She'd miss him, their time together and the sex, of course, but it was better to get out now, while she still could.

The security of her emotional well-being depended on the strength of her resolve and, as she finally drifted off into an uneasy sleep, she vowed that no matter how mighty the battle Leo mounted, how ruthlessly he blocked her protests, she would not waver. However hard she had to fight him, and quite possibly herself, in the morning, she absolutely *would* leave.

CHAPTER ELEVEN

AFTER A RESTLESS NIGHT, Willow woke early, her eyes gritty as if filled with sand, her chest tight as if caught in a vice. She got up and packed her things, which had moved to the spare room with her, ignoring the voice in her head that lamented the way things had to be and the strange aching of her heart. Leaving was the right thing, the only thing, to do, she reminded herself over and over again. She had no choice if she wanted to avoid misery and destruction.

Steeling herself against weakness, armed for battle, she picked up her suitcase and carried it downstairs. She found Leo in the kitchen, sitting at the table, drinking a cup of coffee. He looked exhausted. Tense. Remote. As if recent events had been as tough on him as they had on her.

'Good morning,' he said gruffly.

At the strange lack of expression in his voice,

a shiver rippled down her spine and her throat constricted for a second, but she wouldn't question what might be behind it. She could not afford to get sidetracked. She had to focus on the goal. 'Good morning.'

'Coffee?' he asked with a nod in the direction of the stove.

'No, thank you.'

'How are you feeling?'

'Much better.'

'I'm glad to hear it.'

'Thank you for all your support.'

The smile he gave her was brief. Humourless. 'No problem.'

A horribly wintry silence fell, during which all she could hear was the thundering of her heart. Then Leo opened his mouth to speak and Willow immediately focused, needing to get in first, before she lost her nerve. 'So I'd like to go home now,' she blurted, the words exiting her mouth with a rush.

He started, the porcelain of his cup hitting the marble tabletop with a clatter, his eyebrows shooting up. 'What?'

She took a deep breath to calm down, and braced herself. 'This has been a lot of fun,' she began before amending, 'well, not the last few days, of course, but before that. It's been great. However, real life calls. I need to check on my father. I have things to sort things out before starting work on my next commission and roots to touch up.'

'Seriously?'

'Yes.'

He frowned. Then gave a short nod. 'OK.'

And now the surprise was all hers. He agreed? Just like that? Without a fight? 'Really?' she said, totally confused by his acquiescence when not all that long ago he'd resolutely thwarted her attempts to go.

'I should be heading back to work too,' he said, pushing back his chair and getting to his feet. 'I've neglected the business for longer than I intended. Too long, in hindsight.'

At the trace of irritation she could hear in his voice, Willow flushed with embarrassment and flooded with awkwardness. 'That's my fault,' she said, shifting her weight from one foot to the other, the regret that she hadn't been strong enough to overcome temptation and leave as planned abject. 'I'm sorry.'

He put the cup in the sink. 'Don't be. It's not your fault.'

'You stayed because of me.'

'I gave you little choice.'

'Are you going because of me, too?'

He spun round. His gaze collided with hers, sharp, questioning, and she wished she hadn't said anything because this was not the time to show weakness even if she did, for some reason, badly need to know. 'What do you mean?'

'Do you really have to return to Athens?'

'Yes,' he said. 'Zander messaged me last night. The merger's been causing problems.'

'So it's not because the last few days were a bit too... I don't know...visceral?'

'Absolutely not,' he said, his eyes suddenly blazing with such conviction that she had to believe him. 'Never think that. If anything, know that I am blown away by your strength and resilience.'

'OK, then,' she said, the relief oddly overwhelming.

'When do you want to leave?'

She resisted the urge to tell him she'd changed her mind and she didn't want to leave ever, because she couldn't change her mind. She had to be strong. So she ignored the odd ache in her chest and the tightness of her throat, nodded once, and said, firmly, 'I'm ready to go now.'

The journey back to Athens could not have been more different to the one out. The tension that filled the car was stony not sizzling, and there was no champagne on the plane. They did not exchange long smouldering looks filled with the promise of passion and adventure. They barely looked at each other.

The minute they boarded, Leo attached himself to his phone while Willow sat back and stared out of the window, stifling the dangerous emotions that were clamouring to be acknowledged. Her heart beat fast and her head buzzed beneath the pressure, but she counted down the minutes and kept her mouth shut.

On landing, they disembarked in silence. On the tarmac, she didn't throw herself into his arms and indulge in one last kiss. She didn't break down and beg him to convince her she was wrong about everything. She simply said a cool goodbye, turned on her heel and walked off in the opposite direction, all the while reminding herself she'd had a very lucky escape indeed.

'So what's up?'

Three weeks after Leo's return to the city, Zander emerged onto the roof terrace of Leo's Athens penthouse apartment and set down two bottles of beer on the table.

'Nothing's up,' Leo muttered, pulling one

towards him, wiping his thumb over the condensation and wishing it was as easy to swipe a path through the chaos of his thoughts.

His brother sat down and stretched out his legs. 'You've been like a bear with a sore head ever since you came back from Santorini. Everyone's terrified of you. Especially Maria. She said she's never known you to be like this in all the years she's been your assistant. She even said she preferred me, which means things must be really bad.'

'Tough few weeks,' Leo replied, focusing on the view to avoid his brother's unusually probing gaze. 'It happens.'

'Not to you,' came the dry reply. 'And they haven't been that tough.'

Irritatingly, Zander was right, on both fronts. Generally, when there was an issue at work Leo simply upped his degree of control until it passed, and there'd be far less to catch up on than he'd anticipated, thanks to his brother's eminent capability. He didn't know why he was so on edge and off balance. His usual method of simply burying his concerns and focusing didn't seem to be working.

'So what's this, then?' he asked, indicating the beer with a casual wave of his hand. 'An intervention?'

'Yes. On behalf of all of us. We want to know what's going on.'

His siblings had been discussing him? He didn't much like that either. 'I don't know what you're talking about,' he snapped, opting for denial, hoping against hope his brother would take the hint and leave it.

'Willow Jacobs,' Zander replied, annoyingly doing neither.

At the mention of her name, Leo went still. He clenched his jaw and pushed back the memories that were now trying to barge their way into his head. He would not think of her. Whenever he did, his head spun and his chest tightened. He had no idea why. Yet his brother required some sort of response. 'What about her?'

'Are you in love with her?'

His heart skipped a beat and then began to race, but he drew in a deep breath of warm evening air and forced himself to calm down. 'Don't be ridiculous.'

'I saw the photos,' said Zander. '*Everyone* saw the photos.'

Leo shuddered.

'Olympia said she could see it in your eyes.'

'Olympia is mistaken.'

'You staked a claim on her the night of

Daph's wedding,' Zander pointed out unhelpfully. 'I've never known you to do that sort of thing before.'

No, well, he'd lost his mind for a while. But he had it back now. The merger was on track. Lazlo appeared to be keeping their mother under control. The status quo had resumed. Exactly as he'd planned. He hadn't even had to work for it. By announcing her intention to go home that last morning on Santorini, Willow had made it unexpectedly easy for him. It was therefore absurd to feel rejected. At the airport, he'd watched her walk away and he'd been relieved. Not gutted like a fish. *Relieved.* She had the potential to bring out the absolute worst in him. He'd had a very lucky escape.

'It was a blip,' he said flatly. 'A lapse of sanity. It's over.'

'That seems a shame.'

'What would you know about it?'

'Very little, I have to admit. Our parents didn't exactly set a fine example. But look at Daphne and Ari. Where love exists it's a beautiful thing. You did look happy and relaxed with her in those photos.'

No. He hadn't. He hadn't looked anything in those photos, and he was done talking about it.

'I thought you wanted to discuss business,'

he said, shifting round and fixing Zander with his iciest glare.

'That's right.'

'Well?'

'Do you genuinely enjoy running the company?' his brother asked, unfortunately not remotely fazed by the glare. 'Because I do. So if you don't, I'd be more than happy to take over permanently.'

Take over? What the hell? That wasn't happening. He would not abdicate the responsibilities his father had given him. He would not fail.

'I'm fine,' Leo said through gritted teeth, a thumping headache beginning to develop at his right temple. 'Everything is absolutely fine.'

A week later however, Leo had to admit it wasn't fine. Something was very wrong indeed. He wasn't sleeping. He wasn't eating. And his behaviour at the office had gone from bad to worse. He was snapping people's heads off and snarling at anyone who got in his way. Zander had ordered him to stay at home before everyone jumped ship, and despite immensely disliking being told what to do, Leo had grudgingly agreed for the sake of the business.

Unfortunately, however, all that meant was that he had time on his hands in which to do nothing by prowl round his apartment, struggling and failing to keep a lid on the bubbling emotions seething away deep inside him and the thoughts generated by the conversation he'd had with his brother on the terrace whirling around his brain on some interminable loop.

He'd never considered stepping down before. He'd never even dared take a break until six weeks or so ago. To not continue his father's legacy—the destiny that had been drummed into him practically from birth—would be a betrayal he could not contemplate.

But as he stalked into the kitchen to make himself the fourth coffee of the day even though it was only nine in the morning, he wondered if perhaps he was too close to be able to see the situation objectively.

What would an outsider think? What would Willow think? She'd had a few pertinent ideas about roles and responsibilities—not that she crossed his mind much. She'd be the first to tell him to stand aside and install Zander as CEO, and she'd be right. Because while Leo merely endured the position, his brother had relished it. He had a knack with people and was insanely driven. He was ruthless and brilliant. He'd always been the better man for the job.

He was also annoyingly perceptive because

while Leo liked to tell himself that he rarely thought about Willow, the truth was that she was in his head all the damn time. She ruined his sleep. She disrupted his train of thought. He missed her more than he'd ever thought possible.

Could he have done the unthinkable and fallen in love with her?

In response to the question that flashed through his mind, Leo froze, ground coffee spilling all over the worktop.

No. He couldn't. It was impossible. He'd sworn not to allow it.

And yet, when he ran through all the reasons she was wrong for him, he was suddenly able to counteract every single one of them. Streakless hair and unadorned ears now seemed dull. Far from fearing her influence, he *wanted* to hear her views and seek her input. He wasn't destructive like his mother. He wasn't weak like his father when it came to the personal. He had nothing to fear from emotion. The days he'd spent with Willow on Santorini, he'd felt alive, for the first time in years. Free from burden. Free to be himself. She'd made him feel invincible. The world wouldn't collapse if he wasn't in control of it 24-7. It hadn't when he'd been away. And as for betraying his father's legacy, surely he'd be preserving it by putting the best person in charge.

As the foundations of his existence fell away, so too did the walls around his heart. He did love Willow, he realised with a jolt as unleashed emotions began to batter him on all sides, stealing the breath from his lungs and draining the strength from his limbs so sharply he had to fumble for a chair. He probably had from the moment she'd stood up to him by the pool the afternoon they'd met. Why else would he have pursued her when every fibre of his being had warned him away? He'd dressed it up as guilt, the righting of wrongs, but fundamentally he'd just wanted her.

And he still did.

When he thought of his life without her, bleak, colourless, empty, it chilled him to the bone. When he counted the days and thought of her going through another period alone and in pain, it clawed at his chest. He wanted to protect her, support her, love her until the day he died, which with any luck would be decades from now.

So what was he going to do about it?

And more importantly, given her fears about love, would she ever let him?

Willow had spent the time she'd been back in London principally thanking her lucky stars that she'd escaped Leo's powerful and potentially destructive orbit when she had.

Determined to consign her sojourn on Santorini to history, to wipe him from her head, she filled her diary with visits to her father and arrangements with her friends. She replenished her art materials, had new violet streaks put in her hair and updated her website to include the portrait of Selene and the stunningly positive press that it had generated.

She didn't think about Leo. She didn't wonder what he was doing or how he was and she didn't even contemplate clicking on the links to some apparently gossipy articles that a friend had forwarded. She certainly didn't fish out the sketchbooks stuffed with drawings of him that she'd stashed at the back of a drawer, flick through them and reminisce. Nor, when her period hit again, did she wish someone would give her a backrub and run her a bath. She just got on with things as she always had and always would.

So life was fine. Uneventful, safe, exactly as she wanted it. The sun was shining and London, with its population basking in the fine weather and spilling out of bars and into parks, looked great. She was busy as a bee, preparing to travel to Milan to paint one of the Italian countesses she'd met at that wedding reception all those weeks ago, and excited about getting back to work. She'd dodged a bullet with regards to feelings, and everything was great.

Until one morning a month after she'd returned, when she was rummaging in the drawer for a pencil, she caught sight of a loose sketch of Leo lying sprawled across the bed in Santorini, and it hit her like a blow to the stomach that nothing was great, that everything was, in fact, pretty bloody awful.

Clutching the drawing, pain slicing though her chest like a knife, Willow sank to the sofa and curled up in a ball, the tears she'd managed to keep at bay for weeks breaching the dam and streaming down her cheeks.

Who had she been kidding? Life might be uneventful and safe but it wasn't what she wanted at all. The sun was shining and the city buzzed, but over *her* head was an oppressively thick black cloud that threatened rain. The thought of Milan and getting back to work was the opposite of thrilling.

She missed Leo so much. More than she'd ever thought possible. She missed his smile and the way he'd looked at her as if trying to seek out every one of her hopes and fears. She wanted him badly and not just because he'd shown her pleasure, adventure and taken such good care of her. She'd loved talking to and arguing with him. He was endlessly fascinating and the days they'd lived like a couple had been the best of her life.

So much for keeping her heart safe. It had been at risk from the moment they'd met. If their relationship really had been purely physical, as she'd so foolishly believed, she wouldn't have wanted things she ought not to want. She wouldn't have done things she'd known were unwise. She'd paid lip service to preventing it, but she'd fallen head over heels in love with him regardless. She loved everything about him.

And it was a disaster. Because Leo did not feel the same way about her. He didn't want her. He cared about her—or he had once upon a time—but he didn't love her. How ironic to have overcome the obstacles that had tormented her for years by falling for someone unavailable.

She hadn't had a lucky escape at all, she thought miserably, a fresh wave of wretchedness washing over her. She should have stayed and fought. For him. For them. She should have persuaded him that she was right for him. Because she was. On paper, yes, they were an unlikely match, but in reality they had a lot in common. They were both ambitious, driven, bound by circumstance. They each had one deceased parent and another not really deserving of the title. She'd never be cool and polished or sophisticated enough to carry off a white trouser suit with any sort of panache, but she believed they understood one another.

If he were by her side she'd have the confidence to overcome her fears and undergo the surgeries. She'd want to do everything in her power to improve her quality of life for herself and for him and to better the possibility of having the children he wanted. She would read the statistics over and over again until she believed them.

She wasn't her father. Leo had been right— she *was* strong and resilient. And yes, something might happen to her, or to him, but then again, it might not. Surely it would be better to have loved and lost than never to have loved at all. Her parents had adored each other. Maybe his continued grief was a price her father was willing to pay for that love.

So what was she going to do about the situation? Was it too late to try and convince Leo that the patterns of the past didn't have to be repeated? Or would she be fighting a losing battle? If she tracked him down and demanded to talk to him, would he be pleased to see her or appalled?

Willow was so wrapped up in misery and confusion that she almost didn't hear the sound of the buzzer. When she did, she grabbed a pillow and stuck it over her head for no one need see her in this much of a state. But whoever it was wasn't going away, so with a deep ragged sigh she threw aside the pillow, levered herself off the sofa and padded to the door.

'Yes?'

'Willow? It's Leo.'

Her heart stopped, then began to gallop. Was she hallucinating? Had she somehow conjured him up with the strength of her feelings? He'd frequently been able to read her mind, but surely telepathy couldn't cross continents. So why was he here?

With shaking fingers, she buzzed him in and estimated she had one minute to make herself presentable, which wasn't nearly enough, but at least her clothes were clean and her recently touched-up hair was good.

She stood at the open door, her entire body vibrating, her limbs alarmingly weak. His thumps up the stairs matched the thundering of her pulse, and then he was striding towards her, big, broad and so handsome he took her breath away, and God, it was good to see him.

'Leo,' she said, the surge of longing that she'd spent a month trying to deny nearly taking out what remained of her knees. 'What are you doing here? You look dreadful.'

He rubbed his hands over his face, which was haggard and more sharply angled, as if he'd lost weight, then shoved them in the pockets of his jeans. 'Can I come in?'

'Of course.' She stood aside to let him pass then closed the door behind him, her studio immediately filling with a restless sort of energy that put every one of her senses on high alert. 'Would you like something to drink?'

'No, thank you,' he said, heading into the space then turning to face her, the intensity of his gaze pinning her to the spot. 'I'd like to know how you've been.'

Willow swallowed hard, her mind racing. How should she respond? What was he thinking? She couldn't tell. His face gave nothing away. Did she dare use this opportunity to find out? She'd had no time to plan. Yet surely she could be brave. She'd blagged her work into exhibitions. She'd secured an invitation to the wedding of the year then pursued Leo across a dance floor and persuaded him to agree to a one-night stand. When she knew what she wanted she went for it, and she might never get another chance.

'I thought I was doing fine,' she said, her mouth dry, nerves nevertheless tangling in the pit of her stomach. 'But I just realised I'm not. You?'

'The same.'

Her head swam. Her heart thudded. Could she dare to hope? 'I'm going to Milan next week,' she said. 'I'm not as excited about it as I should be.'

'I resigned.'

She blinked in shock. 'Resigned?'

'Zander is the new CEO of Stanhope Kallis.'

'What? Why?'

'I'm tired of doing things I don't want to do,' he said, his gaze trained on her face as if nothing else but her existed. 'I'm sick of living by rules that don't make me happy.'

'I see,' she said, not seeing at all. In fact, she was actually feeling a bit dizzy. He was taking up too much space, too much air. 'So what are you going to do?'

'I haven't decided yet.'

'That must be a concern.'

'You'd think so, wouldn't you?' he said with the ghost of a smile. 'But oddly enough, it isn't.

I feel liberated. As if the weight of the world has been lifted from my shoulders.'

'Then it was the right thing to do.'

'I think so. And do you know what *does* make me happy?'

Right now she knew nothing. She wanted him so much she could barely think straight and this conversation was not proving easy to follow. 'Sailing?'

He shook his head. 'You do.'

She stared at him, reeling. She had to clutch the back of a chair for support. 'What?'

'You make me happy, Willow,' he said, taking his hands out of his pockets as he took a step towards her, his gaze softening. 'When I'm with you there's nowhere else I'd rather be. When I'm not with you, you're all I think about. I'm in love with you. I think I fell for you the moment you challenged me to a compromise by the pool the afternoon I failed to bribe you into not exhibiting your portrait of my mother. Despite what both you and I might have thought, you've turned out to be exactly my type. I've been wrong to fear emotion. I've put too great a value on control. But I am neither of my parents and from now on I intend to forge my own path. I'd like to do it with you.'

He stopped, clearly waiting for a response,

but Willow couldn't speak. Her throat was too tight. Her thoughts were spinning too fast. What he'd just said… It was everything she'd hoped for. If she hadn't been able to feel the emotion pouring off him and see it blazing in his eyes, she'd have thought she were dreaming.

'Are you sure?' she managed eventually, her heart crashing against her ribs so hard she feared one might break.

'I've never been more certain of anything.'

'I might not be able to have children.'

'I know that,' he said simply. 'But I just want you. I believe in us, and I badly want the future we could have, whatever shape that takes. I know that love terrifies you and I understand why. I'm here to convince you to reconsider.'

His sincerity swept away the last of her reservations and love and joy rushed through her, hot, fast and free. 'There's no need,' she said shakily, releasing her grip on the chair and closing the distance between them.

He paled. 'Why not?'

She took his hands in hers and held them tight. 'Because love doesn't terrify me anymore,' she said around the small hot lump in her throat. 'Well, it does a bit, but I've recently realised that I've spent too long living in fear of something that will likely never happen. Too long living with pain that could be so much less. I don't want to be shackled to the past any longer, Leo. I want to look to the future and I want you in it.' She took a deep breath. 'Because I love you, too.'

The colour returned to his face. The tension eased from his shoulders and his eyes bore into hers. 'You do?'

'So much,' she said, losing herself in their swirling depths, the heat of his body and moving in closer. 'You're everything I never dared allow myself to dream of. Everything I thought I could never have. I want to laugh with you, argue with you, grow old with you. I want it all.'

'Then you'd better marry me.'

As he drew her into his arms, a small smile playing around his mouth, joy exploded through her, dizzying her with its intensity, swelling her heart with sheer happiness. 'Yes, please,' she said with the brightest of grins and lifted her head for his kiss.

EPILOGUE

Three years later

LEO HAD SPENT quite a bit of time in hospitals over the last couple of years. With immense courage and impressive persistence, Willow had faced and vanquished her demons and had finally elected to have the surgery that the medical professionals believed would help her.

Hating to see her in continued pain, Leo had been keen to get on with the process once the decision had been made. Willow, however, citing professionalism and her reputation, had refused to let the clients she'd already had booked in down and, as she'd pointed out, the new business he'd set up required as much of his focus as he could give because luxury yachts didn't design, build and charter themselves.

The first operation had taken place twelve months after she'd agreed to marry him, two weeks after they'd actually wed in a small ceremony held at the church around the corner from her father's house so that he could attend.

Before, during and after that and each subsequent one, he'd been there for her every step of the way, doing his best to allay the fears that occasionally surged and reminding her how much he loved her. Despite the disapproval of the surgical team, he'd been at her side both when she went to sleep and when she woke up every single time.

It hadn't been an easy ride, by any means, but every moment of the torment they'd suffered together had been worth it because while the pain hadn't completely disappeared, Willow was no longer wrenched apart one week in every four. She could smile and laugh and function, and the relief and happiness this gave him expanded his heart until it felt too big for his chest.

This particular wing of the private Athens hospital and the carpeted corridor along which he was currently pacing were unfamiliar to him, but the emotions tearing through him weren't. The gut-wrenching terror. The gnawing impatience. The heart-thumping hope. They were nothing new, even if the circumstances were.

What was going on in there? he wondered

grimly as he shoved his hands through his hair and glanced at his watch. It had been hours. Why was it taking so long? If he didn't get an update soon, heads would roll.

'Mr Stanhope?'

In response to the voice behind him Leo came to an abrupt halt and whirled round, nearly colliding with the doctor who was holding open the door. 'Yes?'

'You can go in now.'

He didn't need telling twice. With a muttered thank you, he barged past the doctor and strode across the lobby. He pushed opened the door to Willow's room and there she was, lying in the bed, looking exhausted, frazzled and lovelier than ever.

'Are you all right?' he asked, his heart turning over as it did every time he saw her.

Her eyes shone. Her smile was wide. His gaze dropped to the bundle in her arms and his throat tightened and his vision swam.

'Come and meet our beautiful baby girl.'

* * * * *

Caught up in the intensity of
Virgin's Night with the Greek?
*Make sure to look out for the next instalment
of the Heirs to a Greek Empire series,
coming soon!*

*In the meantime, check out these other stories
by Lucy King!*

The Secrets She Must Tell
Invitation from the Venetian Billionaire
The Billionaire without Rules
Undone by Her Ultra-Rich Boss
Stranded with My Forbidden Billionaire

Available now!